50% OFF!

CBEST ONLINE TEST PREP COURSE

We consider it an honor and a privilege that you chose our CBEST Study Guide. As a way of showing our appreciation and to help us better serve you, we have partnered with Mometrix Test Preparation to offer you 50% off their online CBEST Prep Course.

Mometrix has structured their online course to perfectly complement your printed study guide. Many CBEST courses are needlessly expensive and don't deliver enough value. With their course, you get access to the best CBEST prep material, and you only pay half price.

WHAT'S IN THE CBEST TEST PREP COURSE?

- ✓ **CBEST Study Guide**: Get access to content that complements your study guide.

- ✓ **Progress Tracker**: Their customized course allows you to check off content you have studied or feel confident with.

- ✓ **700+ Practice Questions**: With 700+ practice questions and lesson reviews, you can test yourself again and again to build confidence.

- ✓ **CBEST Flashcards**: Their course includes a flashcard mode consisting of over 570 content cards to help you study.

TO RECEIVE THIS DISCOUNT, VISIT THE WEBSITE AT

link.mometrix.com/cbest

USE THE DISCOUNT CODE:
STARTSTUDYING

IF YOU HAVE ANY QUESTIONS OR CONCERNS, PLEASE CONTACT MOMETRIX AT SUPPORT@MOMETRIX.COM

Free DVD **FREE** Free DVD

Essential Test Tips Video from Trivium Test Prep

Dear Customer,

Thank you for purchasing from Trivium Test Prep! Whether you're looking to join the military, get into college, or advance your career, we're honored to be a part of your journey.

To show our appreciation (and to help you relieve a little of that test-prep stress), we're offering a **FREE *CBEST Essential Test Tips* Video** by Trivium Test Prep. Our video includes 35 test preparation strategies that will help keep you calm and collected before and during your big exam. All we ask is that you email us your feedback and describe your experience with our product. Amazing, awful, or just so-so: we want to hear what you have to say!

To receive your **FREE *CBEST Essential Test Tips* Video**, please email us at 5star@ triviumtestprep.com. Include "Free 5 Star" in the subject line and the following information in your email:

1. The title of the product you purchased.

2. Your rating from 1 – 5 (with 5 being the best).

3. Your feedback about the product, including how our materials helped you meet your goals and ways in which we can improve our products.

4. Your full name and shipping address so we can send your **FREE *CBEST Essential Test Tips* Video**.

If you have any questions or concerns please feel free to contact us directly at 5star@triviumtestprep.com.

Thank you, and good luck with your studies!

CBEST Study Guide 2024-2025

3 Practice Tests and CBEST Prep Book for the California Exam [6th Edition]

Eric Canizales

TABLE OF CONTENTS

Introduction...1

    What is the CBEST? 1

    What's on the CBEST? 1

    How is the CBEST scored? 2

    How is the CBEST administered? 3

    About Cirrus Test Prep 3

    About This Guide 3

1. Reading Skills 4

    Introduction.. 4

    The Main Idea 5

    Supporting Details 7

    Facts and Opinions.. 9

    Making Inferences 10

    Understanding the Author 12

    Meaning of Words and Phrases 18

    Comparing Passages 28

    Text Features 30

    Answer Key 31

2. Mathematics 33

    Estimation, Measurement, and Statistical Principles 33

    Computation and Problem Solving 45

    Numerical and Graphic Relationships 57

    Answer Key 63

3. Writing 69

    Writing A Thesis Statement 69

Structuring the Essay 70

Providing Supporting Evidence 72

Writing Well 73

Practice Test #1 75

Reading 75

Mathematics 91

Writing 104

Answer Key #1 109

Reading 109

Mathematics 112

Writing 120

Practice Test #2 123

Reading 123

Writing 138

Math 143

Answer Key #2 154

Reading 154

Writing 157

Math 159

Practice Test #3 166

ONLINE RESOURCES

Trivium includes online resources with the purchase of this study guide to help you fully prepare for the exam.

Flash Cards

Trivium's flash cards allow you to review important terms easily on your computer or smartphone.

Cheat Sheets

Review the core skills you need to master the exam with easy-to-read Cheat Sheets.

From Stress to Success

Watch "From Stress to Success," a brief but insightful YouTube video that offers the tips, tricks, and secrets experts use to score higher on the exam.

Feedback

Send us helpful feedback!

Access these materials at: **cirrustestprep.com/cbest-online-resources**

Introduction

Congratulations on choosing to take the California Basic Educational Skills Test (CBEST)! By purchasing this book, you've taken the first step toward becoming a teacher, an enriching and satisfying career.

This guide will provide you with a detailed overview of the California Basic Educational Skills Test (CBEST) so you know exactly what to expect on test day. It will prepare you for all three of the sections: the Reading section, the Mathematics section, and the Writing section. We'll take you through all the concepts covered on these tests and give you the opportunity to test your knowledge with practice questions. Even if it's been a while since you last took a major test, don't worry; we'll make sure you're more than ready!

What is the CBEST?

The CBEST is used in the state of California to measure teacher candidates' aptitude in mathematics, reading, language skills, and writing. You may take the sections individually on separate dates, or you may take them all on the same date; either way you must complete all three sections in order to pass the exam. While you may also be required to take other tests developed or approved by the California Commission on Teacher Credentialing (CTC) for specific academic subjects, the core subjects tested on the CBEST are essential for anyone entering the teaching profession.

What's on the CBEST?

The CBEST gauges college-level mathematics, reading, and writing skills. Each section—Mathematics, Reading, and Writing—is broken down into different categories based on the skills needed to succeed in a teacher preparation program.

The mathematics section focuses on estimation, measurement, statistical principles, problem solving, computation, and numerical and graphic relationships. You may not use a calculator.

On the Reading section, you will read and answer questions concerning passages about varying topics. Expect to analyze tables and graphs as well. The section addresses critical analysis and evaluation, and research and comprehension. Questions test your critical thinking, analytical, and research skills as well as reading comprehension.

On the Writing section, you must write two essays responding to two topics. In one, you will be provided with a specific statement or situation, which you must analyze. In the other essay, you will be asked to discuss a personal experience. The Writing section measures your language and compositional skills.

You are always allotted four hours for the CBEST whether you take one, two, or all three sections. You may choose which sections to take and how many; regardless of your choices, you will have four hours during which you will divide and manage your time. This time period includes fifteen minutes to complete a nondisclosure agreement and tutorial.

What's on the California Basic Educational Skills Test (CBEST)?			
Section	Concepts	Number of Questions	Time
Mathematics	Estimation, measurement, and statistical principles; computation and problem solving; and numerical and graphical relationships	50 multiple-choice questions	
Reading	Critical analysis and evaluation; comprehension and research skills	50 multiple-choice questions	
Writing	Purpose, audience, text structure, argument or claim, supporting details, language skills	2 essays	
Total		100 multiple-choice questions and 2 essays	4 hours (allotted for test time regardless of number of sections you take)

How is the CBEST scored?

Your preliminary scores for the Reading and Mathematics sections are immediately available upon completion. Official scores are released up to two weeks after taking the test. It can take up to an additional two weeks to receive your Writing scores. Once your scores are posted, they will only remain available for sixty days. Your CBEST scores will automatically be sent to the California Department of Education's Bureau of Educator Certification; however, to have them sent to a college or university, you must make a request when you register for the exam.

Each multiple-choice question is worth one raw point. The total number of questions you answer correctly is added up to obtain your raw score. Your raw score is then scaled; a minimum scaled score of 123 is required to pass the CBEST. Scaled scores for individual sections range from 20 to 80. A scaled score of 41 is required to pass individual sections of the test; however, you may pass the whole CBEST with a scaled score of 37 on one or two sections if your total score is 123 or more. If any section is *below* 37, though, you will not pass.

Keep in mind that a small number of multiple-choice questions are experimental and will not count toward your overall score. ETS uses these to test out new questions for future exams. However, as those questions are not indicated on the test, you must respond to every question.

There is no penalty for guessing on the CBEST, so be sure to eliminate answer choices and answer every question. If you still do not know the answer, guess; you may get it right!

How is the CBEST administered?

The CBEST is both computer- and paper-based. The computer-based test is offered continuously at a range of universities and testing centers. The paper-based test is offered approximately every three months. It may be taken in its individual parts or all at once. Check http://ctcexams.nesinc.com for more information. You will need to print your registration ticket from your online account and bring it, along with your identification, to the testing site on test day. No pens, pencils, erasers, or calculators are allowed. If you are taking the computer-based test, you will be provided with a pen and scratch paper to take notes or prepare your responses to the Writing section.

About Cirrus Test Prep

Cirrus Test Prep study guides are designed by current and former educators and are tailored to meet your needs as an incoming educator. Our guides offer all of the resources necessary to help you pass teacher certification tests across the nation.

Cirrus clouds are graceful, wispy clouds characterized by their high altitude. Just like cirrus clouds, Cirrus Test Prep's goal is to help educators "aim high" when it comes to obtaining their teacher certification and entering the classroom.

About This Guide

This guide will help you master the most important test topics and also develop critical test-taking skills. We have built features into our books to prepare you for your tests and increase your score. Along with a detailed summary of the test's format, content, and scoring, we offer an in-depth overview of the content knowledge required to pass the test. Our sidebars provide interesting information, highlight key concepts, and review content so that you can solidify your understanding of the exam's concepts. Test your knowledge with Practice Questions and detailed answer explanations in the text that help you think through the problems on the exam, and with two full-length practice tests that reflect the content and format of the CBEST. We're pleased you've chosen Cirrus to be a part of your professional journey!

1. Reading Skills

Introduction

The Reading Test assesses overall proficiency in several key reading skills, including building inferences, understanding themes, and describing the organization and craft of writing.

The test has fifty multiple-choice questions. Questions follow a brief passage of text or media, such as a graph. The number of questions following each passage depends on how long the passage is: four to seven questions follow a 200-word passage or a pair of passages; three questions follow a 100-word passage; and single questions follow statements and briefer passages. Question stems may appear as fill-in-the-blank sentences, straightforward questions, or *LEAST/NEVER/EXCEPT* questions, which ask the reader to choose the answer that does not fit. Several strategies and terms are discussed in the following sections and throughout this book.

Comprehension and Context

This category focuses on the text as a whole. The questions ask for explanations of the main ideas and how they lead to inferences and conclusions. Look for connections between sections of the text as well as consistency and meaning of the author's argument. Test takers should also identify and accurately summarize the theme by giving details that support the author's argument.

Strategies for approaching this type of question include previewing the questions and outlining. Reading through the questions before reading the passage is a good way for students to find a focus. The questions describe what to look for, and students can rule out wrong answer choices by finding the main ideas and supporting details. Students can outline the text by jotting down words or phrases that describe the main idea of each paragraph and underlining important details that support that idea.

Other questions may require relating the details of a passage to the overall organization and meaning of that passage. These questions ask for evaluations of specific areas of the text as they relate to the author's purpose and argument, and descriptions of how the author uses specific words, figurative language, or transitions.

For these questions, the best strategy entails returning to the passage after reading each question and looking for the specific context and location of each question. Marking wrong answers and circling the important aspects of the question stem and answer are also helpful strategies.

Research and Reference Skills

These questions test your ability to use text tools like tables of contents, headings, and indexes to find information. You may be asked to assess a text, alternative texts like a table of contents or index, or visual media like a graph or chart.

Determining what to pay attention to is accomplished by reviewing each question before reading its relative passage and returning to the passage as needed. A passage with media such as visuals requires the same skills as reading text. Readers should consider each question to determine the skills and knowledge needed to answer it. Deconstructing the question stem reveals what sort of question it is.

The Main Idea

Identifying the Main Idea

The main idea of a text is the argument the author is making about a particular topic. Every sentence in a passage should support or address the main idea in some way. To identify the main idea, first identify the topic. The difference between the two is simple: the **topic** is the overall subject matter of a passage; the **main idea** is what the author wants to say about that topic.

Consider a political election. A candidate is running for office and plans to deliver a speech asserting her position on tax reform, which is that taxes should be lowered. The topic of the speech is tax reform, and the main idea is that taxes should be lowered. The candidate is going to say this in her speech and support it with examples proving why lowering taxes would benefit the public and how it could be accomplished.

Other candidates may have different perspectives on the same topic. They may think higher taxes are necessary or current taxes are adequate. Their speeches, while on the same topic of tax reform, would probably have different main ideas supported by different examples and evidence.

> **HELPFUL HINT**
>
> **Topic:** the subject of the passage.
> **Main idea:** the argument the writer is making about the topic.

Read the following passage and identify the topic and main idea.

Babe Didrikson Zaharias, one of the most decorated female athletes of the twentieth century, is an inspiration for everyone. Born in 1911 in Beaumont, Texas, Zaharias lived in a time when women were considered second class to men, but she never let that stop her from becoming a champion. Zaharias was one of seven children in a poor immigrant family and was competitive from an early age. As a child she excelled at most things she tried, especially sports, which continued into high school and beyond. After high school, Zaharias played amateur basketball for two years, and soon after began training in track and field. Despite the fact that women were only allowed to enter in three events, Zaharias represented the United States in the 1932 Los Angeles Olympics, and won two gold medals and one silver in track and field events.

The topic of this paragraph is obviously Babe Zaharias—the whole passage describes events from her life. Determining the main idea, however, requires a little more analysis. To figure out the main idea, ask what the writer is saying about Zaharias. The writer describes Zaharias as an inspiration and talks about the hardships she overcame and her many accomplishments. These details support the writer's main idea: Babe Zaharias is an accomplished and inspirational woman.

Fictional works may have a theme instead of a main idea. A **theme** is an idea or perspective that emerges from the way a literary work engages with its topic. For example, a central topic in F. Scott Fitzgerald's novel *The Great Gatsby* is money: the characters are all defined by their relative wealth. The theme of the novel is what Fitzgerald is trying to say about money: that being extremely wealthy leads to excess and moral decay.

1. Reading Skills

Practice Question

The Battle of the Little Bighorn, commonly called Custer's Last Stand, was a battle between the Lakota, the Northern Cheyenne, the Arapaho, and the Seventh Cavalry Regiment of the US Army. Led by war leaders Crazy Horse and Chief Gall and the religious leader Sitting Bull, the allied tribes of the Plains Indians decisively defeated their US foes. Two hundred and sixty-eight US soldiers were killed, including General George Armstrong Custer, two of his brothers, his nephew, his brother-in-law, and six Indian scouts.

1) What is the main idea of this passage?
   A. Most of General Custer's family died in the Battle of the Little Bighorn.
   B. Crazy Horse and Chief Gall were important leaders of the Plains Indians.
   C. The Seventh Cavalry Regiment was formed to fight Native American tribes.
   D. Sitting Bull and George Custer were fierce enemies.
   E. The Battle of the Little Bighorn was a significant victory for the Plains Indians.

In 1953, doctors surgically removed the hippocampus of patient Henry Molaison in an attempt to stop his frequent seizures. Unexpectedly, he lost the ability to form new memories, leading to the biggest breakthrough in the science of memory. Molaison's long-term memory—of events more than a year before his surgery—was unchanged, as was his ability to learn physical skills. From this, scientists learned that different types of memory are handled by different parts of the brain, with the hippocampus responsible for **episodic memory**, the shortterm recall of events. They have since discovered that some memories are then channeled to the cortex, the outer layers of the brain that handle higher functions, where they are gradually integrated with related information to build lasting knowledge about our world.

2) The main idea of the passage is that
   A. Molaison's surgery posed significant risk to the functioning of his brain.
   B. short-term and long-term memory are stored in different parts of the brain.
   C. long-term memory forms over a longer period than short-term memory.
   D. memories of physical skills are processed differently than memories of events.
   E. the hippocampus stores all memories related to events.

Topic and Summary Sentences

The topic, and sometimes the main idea of a paragraph, is introduced in the **topic sentence**. The topic sentence usually appears early in a passage. The first sentence in the paragraph about Babe Zaharias states the topic and main idea: "Babe Didrikson Zaharias, one of the most decorated female athletes of the twentieth century, is an inspiration for everyone."

Even though paragraphs generally begin with topic sentences, writers sometimes build up to the topic sentence by using supporting details to generate interest or build an argument. Readers should watch out for paragraphs that do not include a clear topic sentence.

The **summary sentence**, on the other hand, often—but not always—comes at the end of a paragraph or passage, because it wraps up all the ideas presented. This sentence provides an understanding of what the author wants to say about the topic and what conclusions to draw about it.

The topic sentence acts as an introduction to a topic, allowing readers to activate their own ideas and experiences. The summary statement asks readers to accept the author's ideas about that topic. A summary sentence helps readers quickly identify a piece's main idea.

Practice Question

The Constitution of the United States establishes a series of limits to rein in centralized power. "Separation of powers" distributes federal authority among three branches: the executive, the legislative, and the judicial. The system of "checks and balances" prevents any one branch from usurping power. "States' rights" are protected under the Constitution from too much encroachment by the federal government. "Enumeration of powers" names the specific and few powers the federal government has. These four restrictions have helped sustain the American republic for over two centuries.

3) Which of the following is the passage's topic sentence?
    A. These four restrictions have helped sustain the American republic for over two centuries.
    B. The Constitution of the United States establishes a series of limits to rein in centralized power.
    C. "Enumeration of powers" names the specific and few powers the federal government has.
    D. The system of "checks and balances" prevents any one branch from usurping power.
    E. "Separation of powers" distributes federal authority among three branches: the executive, the legislative, and the judicial.

4) Which of the following is the passage's summary sentence?
    A. These four restrictions have helped sustain the American republic for over two centuries.
    B. The Constitution of the United States establishes a series of limits to rein in centralized power.
    C. "Enumeration of powers" names the specific and few powers the federal government has.
    D. The system of "checks and balances" prevents any one branch from usurping power.
    E. "Separation of powers" distributes federal authority among three branches: the executive, the legislative, and the judicial.

Supporting Details

The middle of a paragraph is built with **supporting details**. Supporting details come in many forms. The purpose of the passage dictates the type of details that will support the main idea. A persuasive passage may use facts and data or give specific reasons for the author's opinion. An informative passage will mostly use facts about the topic to support the main idea. Even a narrative passage will have supporting details—specific things the author says to develop the story and characters.

The most important aspect of supporting details is that they support the main idea. Examining supporting details and how they work together will help readers understand the author's view on a topic and the passage's main idea. Supporting details are key to understanding a passage.

How can readers identify the most important information in a passage? Supporting details help pinpoint the main idea, but it is easier to first locate the most important supporting details by understanding the main idea. This way, the pieces that make up the main argument become clear.

Let's look again at the passage about athlete Babe Zaharias.

Babe Didrikson Zaharias, one of the most decorated female athletes of the twentieth century, is an inspiration for everyone. Born in 1911 in Beaumont, Texas, Zaharias lived in a time when women were considered second class to men, but she never let that stop her from becoming a champion. Babe was one of seven children in a poor immigrant family and was competitive from an early age. As a child she excelled at most things she tried, especially sports, which continued into high school and beyond. After high school, Babe played amateur basketball for two years, and soon after began training in track and field. Despite the fact that women were only allowed to enter in three events, Zaharias represented the United States in the 1932 Los Angeles Olympics, and won two gold medals and one silver for track and field events.

The main idea is that Zaharias is someone to admire—an idea introduced in the opening sentence. The rest of the paragraph gives details that support this idea. These details include the circumstances of her childhood, her early success at sports, and the medals she won at the Olympics.

Readers looking for supporting details should watch for signal words. **Signal words** are transitions and conjunctions that explain how one sentence or idea is connected to another. They "signal" that a supporting fact or idea will follow, and so can be helpful in identifying supporting details. These words and phrases can be anywhere in a sentence. Signal words can add information, provide counterarguments, create organization in a passage, or draw conclusions. Some common signal words are "in particular," "in addition," "besides," "in contrast," "therefore," and "because."

Signal words can also help rule out certain sentences as the main idea or topic sentence. If a sentence begins with one of these phrases, it will likely be too specific to be a main idea.

Readers can use supporting details to understand the main idea of a text or support an argument, but they must evaluate these details for relevance and consistency. The author might leave out details that do not directly support the main idea of a text or that support an opposing argument. Readers should think critically about what information authors choose to include or leave out. This is particularly important in persuasive writing, when an author's bias may influence their writing.

Critical reading means being alert for striking features of a text. For example, does a description seem exaggerated or overstated? Do certain words—such as "agonizing"—seem overly emotive? Are rhetorical questions used to lead the reader to a certain conclusion? Bias and audience are discussed later in this chapter (see "Understanding the Author" on page 11).

1. Reading Skills

Practice Question

For thirteen years, a spacecraft called ***Cassini*** was on an exploratory mission to Saturn. The spacecraft was designed not to return but to end its journey by diving into Saturn's atmosphere. This dramatic ending provided scientists with unprecedented information about Saturn's atmosphere and its magnetic and gravitational fields. First, however, ***Cassini*** passed Saturn's largest moon, Titan, where it recorded data on Titan's curious methane lakes, gathering information about potential seasons on the planet-sized moon. Then it passed through the unexplored region between Saturn itself and its famous rings. Scientists hope to learn how old the rings are and to directly examine the particles that make them up. ***Cassini***'s mission ended in 2017, but researchers have new questions for future exploration.

5) According to the passage, scientists want to learn more about Titan's
   A. gravity, based on examination of its magnetic field.
   B. rings, based on the particles that compose them.
   C. seasons, based on changes to its lakes.
   D. age, based on analysis of its minerals and gases.
   E. atmosphere, based on measurements of its gravity.

The study showed that private tutoring gives a significant advantage to those students who are able to afford it. Researchers looked at the grades of students who had received free tutoring through the school versus those whose parents had paid for private tutors. The study included 2500 students in three high schools across four grade levels. The study found that private tutoring corresponded with a rise in grade point average (GPA) of 0.5 compared to students who used the school's free tutor service, and 0.7 compared to students who used no tutoring.

After reviewing the study, the board is recommending that the school restructure its free tutor service to provide a more equitable education for all students.

6) Which of the following would weaken the author's argument?
   A. the fact that the cited study was funded by a company that provides discounted tutoring through schools
   B. a study showing differences in standardized test scores between students at schools in different neighborhoods
   C. a statement signed by local teachers stating that they do not provide preferential treatment in the classroom or when grading
   D. a study showing that GPA does not strongly correlate with success in college
   E. a pricing schedule for private tutors who provided services to students in the study

Facts and Opinions

A **fact** is a piece of information that can be proven true or false. Its truthfulness or falsity cannot be changed, no matter who verifies it. The statement "Wednesday comes after Tuesday" is a fact—anyone can point to a calendar to prove it. An **opinion** is a belief that others may or may not agree with. The assertion "Television is more entertaining than feature films" is an opinion—people will agree or disagree with this statement, and there is no reference to prove or disprove it.

1. Reading Skills

Authors use both facts and opinions as supporting details. They may mix facts with opinions or state an opinion as if it were a fact. The exam may ask readers to differentiate between facts and opinions.

Practice Question

The most important part of brewing coffee is getting the right water. Choose a water that you think has a nice, neutral flavor. Anything with too many minerals or contaminants will change the flavor of the coffee, and water with too few minerals won't do a good job of extracting the flavor from the coffee beans. Water should be heated to between 195 and 205 degrees Fahrenheit. Boiling water (212 degrees Fahrenheit) will burn the beans and give your coffee a scorched flavor.

While the water is heating, grind your beans. Remember, the fresher the grind, the fresher the flavor of the coffee. The number of beans depends on your personal taste. Obviously, more beans will result in a more robust flavor, while fewer beans will give your coffee a more subtle taste. The texture of the grind should not be too fine (which can lead to bitter coffee) or too coarse (which can lead to weak coffee).

Once the beans are ground and the water has reached the perfect temperature, you're ready to brew. A French press (which we recommend) allows you to control brewing time and provide a thorough brew. Pour the grounds into the press, then pour the hot water over the grounds and let it steep. The brew shouldn't require more than five minutes, although if you like your coffee a bit harsher, you can leave it longer. Finally, use the plunger to remove the grounds and pour.

7) Which of the following statements based on the passage should be considered an opinion?
   A. While the water is heating, grind your beans.
   B. A French press (which we recommend) allows you to control brewing time and provide a thorough brew.
   C. Anything with too many minerals or contaminants will change the flavor of the coffee, and water with too few minerals won't do a good job of extracting the flavor from the coffee beans.
   D. Finally, use the plunger to remove the grounds and pour.
   E. Obviously, more beans will result in a more robust flavor, while fewer beans will give your coffee a more subtle taste.

Making Inferences

In addition to understanding the main idea and factual content of a passage, readers should think about other information in a passage. In a nonfiction passage, for example, questions might ask which statement the author would agree with. In a fictional work, readers might be asked to anticipate what a character would do next.

To answer such questions, readers need to understand the topic and main idea of the passage. This information allows the reader to figure out which of the answer choices best fits the criteria (or, alternatively, which do not).

Readers should try to understand the explicit meanings of information or a narrative. This happens when they draw conclusions and make logical inferences. To draw a conclusion, readers consider the details or facts. They then come to a **conclusion**—the next logical point in the thought sequence.

> **HELPFUL HINT**
>
> Readers draw conclusions by thinking about how the author wants them to feel. Some carefully selected facts can cause readers to feel a certain way.

For example, in a Hemingway story, an old man sits alone in a café. A young waiter says that the café is closing, but the old man continues to drink. The waiter starts closing up, and the old man signals for a refill. Based on these details, the reader might conclude that the old man has not understood the waiter's desire for him to leave.

An inference is different from a conclusion. An **inference** is an assumption the reader makes based on details in the text as well as their own knowledge. It is more of an educated guess that extends the literal meaning. Inferences begin with the given details. The reader then uses these to figure out more facts. What the reader already knows informs what is suggested by the details of decisions or situations in the text. In the example above, the reader might infer that the old man is lonely, enjoys being in the café, and is reluctant to leave.

It is important to infer character motivation when reading fictional text. The characters' actions move the plot forward. A series of events is understood by making sense of why the characters did what they did. Hemingway includes contrasting details as the young waiter and an older waiter discuss the old man. The older waiter sympathizes with the old man. Both men have no one at home and experience a sense of emptiness in life, which brings them to the café.

> **DID YOU KNOW?**
>
> When considering a character's motivations, the reader should ask what the character wants to achieve, what the character will get by accomplishing this, and what the character seems to value the most.

Another aspect of understanding text is connecting it to other texts. Readers may connect the Hemingway story about the old man in the café to other Hemingway stories about people dealing with loss and loneliness in a dignified way. They can extend their initial connections to people they know or their personal experiences.

When readers read a persuasive text, they often connect the arguments made to counterarguments and opposing evidence of which they are aware. They use these connections to infer meaning.

Practice Question

Between November 15 and December 21, 1864, Major General William Tecumseh Sherman marched Union troops from the recently captured city of Atlanta to the port of Savannah. The goal was not only to capture the port city and secure Georgia for the Union but also to destroy the Confederacy's infrastructure and demoralize its people. Sherman and his troops destroyed rail lines and burned buildings and fields. They packed only twenty days' worth of rations, foraging for the rest of their supplies from farms along the way. By the time they reached Savannah, they had destroyed 300 miles of railroad and countless cotton gins and mills, and seized 4000 mules, 13,000 head of cattle, 9.5 million pounds of corn, and 10.5 million pounds of fodder. Sherman estimated his troops inflicted $100 million in damages.

8) It can be inferred from the passage that the Confederacy
    A. strongly resisted the actions of Sherman's troops.
    B. was greatly weakened by the destruction.
    C. used the march as a rallying point.
    D. was relatively unaffected by the march.
    E. relied heavily on the port of Savannah.

The cisco, a foot-long freshwater fish native to the Great Lakes, once thrived throughout the basin but had virtually disappeared by the 1950s. Today, however, fishermen are pulling them up by the net-load in Lake Michigan and Lake Ontario. It is highly unusual for a native species to revive, and the reason for the cisco's reemergence is even more unlikely. The cisco have an invasive species, quagga mussels, to thank for their return. Quagga mussels depleted nutrients in the lakes, harming other species highly dependent on these nutrients. Cisco, however, thrive in low-nutrient environments. As other species—many invasive—diminished, cisco flourished in their place.

9) It can be inferred from the passage that most invasive species
    A. support the growth of native species.
    B. do not impact the development of native species.
    C. struggle to survive in their new environments.
    D. cause the decline of native species.
    E. compete with each other for resources.

Understanding the Author

Many questions on the CBEST Reading Test will ask readers to interpret an author's intentions and ideas. This means readers must examine the author's perspective and purpose as well as the way the author uses language to communicate these things.

In every passage, an author chooses words, structures, and content with specific purpose and intent. With this in mind, the reader can understand why an author picks certain words and structures and how these relate to the content.

The Author's Purpose

The author sets out with a specific goal: to communicate a particular idea to an audience. The **author's purpose** is determined by asking why the author wants the reader to understand the passage's main idea. There are four purposes an author might have:

- to entertain the reader
- to persuade the reader of an opinion or argument
- to describe something, such as a person, place, thing, or event
- to explain a process or procedure

Within each of these general purposes, the author may direct the audience to take a clear action or respond in a certain way.

Identifying an author's purpose can be tricky, but the writing itself often gives clues. For example, if an author's purpose is to entertain, the writing may include vivid characters, exciting plot twists, or beautiful, figurative language. On the other hand, if an author wishes to persuade the reader, there may be an argument or convincing examples that support the author's point of view. An author who wishes to describe a person, place, or event may include lots of details as well as plenty of adjectives and adverbs. Finally, the author whose purpose is to explain a process or procedure may include step-by-step instructions or information in a sequence.

There are different **modes** of written materials that are related to an author's purpose. A short story, for example, is meant to entertain, while an online news article is designed to inform the public about a current event. Each type of writing has a specific name:

- Narrative writing tells a story (novel, short story, play).
- Informational or expository writing informs people (newspaper and magazine articles).
- Technical writing explains something (product manual, instructions).
- Persuasive writing tries to convince the reader of something (opinion column or a blog).

The author's purpose for writing a passage is also connected to the structure of that text. In a **narrative**, the author tells a story to illustrate a theme or idea the reader needs to consider. In a narrative, the author uses characteristics of storytelling, such as chronological order, characters, and a defined setting, and these characteristics communicate the author's theme or main idea.

In an **expository** passage, on the other hand, the author simply seeks to explain an idea or topic to the reader. The main idea will probably be a factual statement or a direct assertion of a broadly held opinion. Expository writing can come in many forms, but one essential feature is a fair and balanced representation of a topic. The author may explore one detailed aspect or a broad range of characteristics, but he or she mainly seeks to prompt a decision from the reader.

> **TEACHING TIP**
>
> When reading a persuasive text, students should be aware of what the author believes about the topic.

Similarly, in **technical** writing, the author's purpose is to explain specific processes, techniques, or equipment so the reader can use that process or equipment to get a desired result. Writing like this uses chronological or spatial structures, specialized vocabulary, and imperative or directive language.

In **persuasive** writing, the author seeks to convince the reader to accept an opinion or belief. Much like expository writing, persuasive writing is presented in many organizational forms, but the author uses specific techniques, or **rhetorical strategies**, to build an argument. Readers can identify these strategies to clearly understand what an author wants them to believe, how the author's perspective and purpose may lead to bias, and whether the passage includes any logical fallacies.

Common rhetorical strategies include the appeals to ethos, logos, and pathos. An author uses these to build trust with the reader, to explain the logical points of their argument, and to convince the reader to agree with their opinion.

An **ethos—ethical—appeal** uses balanced, fair language and seeks to build a trusting relationship between the author and the reader. An author might explain their credentials, include the reader in an argument, or offer concessions to an opposing argument.

A **logos—logical—appeal** builds on that trust by providing facts and support for the author's opinion, explaining the argument with clear connections and reasoning. At this point, the reader should beware of logical fallacies that connect unrelated ideas and build arguments on faulty premises. With a logical appeal, an author tries to convince the reader to accept an opinion or belief by showing that not only is it the most logical option, but it also satisfies the reader's emotional reaction to a topic.

A **pathos—emotional—appeal** does not depend on reasonable connections between ideas. Instead, it reminds the reader, through imagery, strong language, and personal connections, that the author's argument aligns with the reader's best interests.

Many persuasive passages use all three rhetorical strategies to appeal to the reader. Clues will help the reader determine many things about a passage, from the author's purpose to the passage's main idea, but understanding an author's purpose is essential to fully understanding the text.

Practice Question

The Gatling gun, a forerunner of the modern machine gun, was an early rapid-fire spring-loaded, hand-cranked weapon. In 1861, Dr. Richard J. Gatling designed the gun to allow one person to fire many shots quickly. His goal was to reduce the death toll of war by decreasing the number of soldiers needed to fight. The gun had a central shaft surrounded by six rotating barrels. A soldier turned a crank, which rotated the shaft. As each barrel reached a particular point in the cycle, it fired, ejected its spent cartridge, and loaded another. During this process, it cooled down, preparing it to fire again. The Gatling gun was first used in combat by the Union Army during the Civil War. However, each gun was purchased directly by individual commanders. The US Army did not purchase a Gatling gun until 1866.

10) The primary purpose of the passage is to
    A. explain why the Gatling gun was harmful to troops.
    B. critique the US Army's use of the Gatling gun.
    C. describe the design and early history of the Gatling gun.
    D. analyze the success of Dr. Gatling in achieving his goals.
    E. compare the Gatling gun to the modern machine gun.

The greatest changes in sensory, motor, and perceptual development happen in the first two years of life. When babies are first born, most of their senses operate in a similar way to those of adults. For example, babies are able to hear before they are born. Studies show that babies turn toward the sound of their mothers' voices just minutes after being born, indicating they recognize the mother's voice from their time in the womb.

The exception to this is vision. A baby's vision changes significantly in the first year of life. Infants initially have a range of vision of only 8 – 12 inches and no depth perception. As a result, they rely primarily on hearing. Vision does not become the dominant sense until babies are around twelve months old. Babies prefer faces to other objects. This preference, along with their limited vision range, means that their sight is initially focused on their caregiver.

11) Which of the following best describes the mode of the passage?
   A. expository
   B. narrative
   C. persuasive
   D. descriptive
   E. rhetorical

Text Structure

The structure of a text determines how the reader understands the argument and how the various details interact to form the argument. Authors can structure passages in several different ways. These distinct organizational patterns, referred to as **text structure**, use the logical relationships between ideas to improve the readability and coherence of a text. The most common ways passages are organized are:

- **problem-solution**: The author outlines a problem and then discusses a solution.

- **comparison-contrast**: The author presents two situations and then discusses the similarities and differences.

- **cause-effect**: The author recounts an action and then discusses the resulting effects.

- **descriptive**: The author describes an idea, object, person, or other item in detail.

- **chronological**: The author describes a situation or tells a story in chronological order.

> **HELPFUL HINT**
>
> Authors often use repetition to reinforce an idea, including repeated words, phrases, or images.

When analyzing a text, the reader should consider how text structure influences the author's meaning. Most important, the reader needs to be aware of how an author emphasizes an idea by the way he or she presents information. For example, including a contrasting idea makes a central idea stand out, and including a series of concrete examples creates a force of facts to support an argument.

Practice Question

The greatest changes in sensory, motor, and perceptual development happen in the first two years of life. When babies are first born, most of their senses operate in a similar way to those of adults. For example, babies are able to hear before they are born. Studies show that babies turn toward the sound of their mothers' voices just minutes after being born, indicating they recognize the mother's voice from their time in the womb.

The exception to this is vision. A baby's vision changes significantly in the first year of life. Infants initially have a range of vision of only 8 – 12 inches and no depth perception. As a result, they rely primarily on hearing. Vision does not become the dominant sense until babies are around twelve months old. Babies prefer faces to other objects. This preference, along with their limited vision range, means that their sight is initially focused on their caregiver.

12) Which term BEST describes the structure of the text?
   A. chronological
   B. cause-effect
   C. problem-solution
   D. comparison-contrast
   E. descriptive

The Audience

The structure, purpose, main idea, and language of a text all converge on one target: the intended audience. An author makes decisions about every aspect of a piece of writing based on that audience, and readers evaluate the writing through the lens of that audience.

By considering the likely reactions of an intended audience, readers can determine many things: whether they are part of that intended audience; the author's purpose for using specific techniques or devices; the biases of the author and how they appear in the writing; and how the author uses rhetorical strategies. While readers evaluate each of these things separately, identifying and considering the intended audience deepens a reader's understanding of a text and helps highlight details.

> **QUICK REVIEW**
>
> A logical argument includes a claim, a reason that supports the claim, and an assumption the reader makes based on accepted beliefs. All parts of the argument need to make sense to the reader, so authors often consider their audience's beliefs as they make their arguments.

Readers can figure out a text's intended audience by asking a few questions. First, what is the main idea of the passage? Who most likely cares about that idea, benefits from it, or needs to know about it? Answering those questions will help reveal the intended audience. For example, if the main idea of a passage is "signs you need to take your car to the mechanic," the audience is probably car owners who do not have a lot of technical knowledge.

Then the reader considers language. The author tailors language to appeal to the intended audience. Readers can understand the audience based on the type of language used. For example, the figurative language John Steinbeck uses in his novel *The Grapes of Wrath* describes the suffering of Americans who migrated to California to find work during the Great Depression of the 1930s.

Steinbeck spoke directly to the Americans who were discriminating against the migrants. Instead of finding work in the "land of milk and honey," migrants faced poverty and injustice. The metaphor that gives the novel its title is "and in the eyes of the people there is the failure; and in the eyes of the hungry there is a growing wrath. In the souls of the people the grapes of wrath are filling and growing heavy, growing heavy for the vintage." Steinbeck used the image of ripening grapes, familiar to those surrounded by vineyards, to condemn the harsh treatment of impoverished migrants and inspire compassion in his audience.

Practice Question

The social and political discourse of America continues to be permeated with idealism. An idealistic viewpoint asserts that the ideals of freedom, equality, justice, and human dignity are the truths that Americans must continue to aspire to. Idealists argue that truth is what should be, not necessarily what is. In general, they work to improve things and to make them as close to ideal as possible.

13) Which phrase BEST describes the author's purpose?
   A. to advocate for freedom, equality, justice, and human rights
   B. to explain what an idealist believes in
   C. to explain what's wrong with social and political discourse in America
   D. to persuade readers to believe in certain truths
   E. to encourage readers to question the truth

Tone and Mood

The **tone** of a passage describes the author's attitude toward the topic. The **mood** is the main feeling or atmosphere in a passage that provokes specific emotions in the reader. The subtle distinction between these two aspects lies in the audience: the mood influences the reader's emotional state in response to the piece, while the tone establishes a relationship between the audience and the author. Does the author want to instruct the audience? Is the author more experienced than the audience? Does the author wish to convey a friendly or equal relationship? In each of these cases, the author uses a different tone to reflect the desired level of communication.

Diction, or word choice, primarily determines mood and tone in a passage. Many readers use only an author's ideas to determine tone. It is better to find specific words from the text and look for patterns in connotation and emotion. By considering categories of words used by the author, the reader can discover the overall emotional atmosphere of a text and the author's attitude toward the subject.

Every word has both a literal meaning and a **connotative meaning**. The latter relies on the common emotions, associations, and experiences an audience might associate with that word. The following words are all synonyms: "dog," "puppy," "cur," "mutt," "canine," "pet." Two of these words—"dog" and "canine"—are neutral words, without strong associations or emotions. Two others—

> **TEACHING TIP**
>
> To determine the author's tone, students should examine what overall feeling they are experiencing.

> **HELPFUL HINT**
>
> To determine the connotation of a word, the reader examines whether it conveys a positive or negative association. Adjectives are often used to influence the reader's feelings, as in the phrase "an ambitious attempt to achieve."

1. Reading Skills

"pet" and "puppy"— have positive associations. The last two—"cur" and "mutt"—have negative associations. A passage that uses one pair of these words versus another pair activates the positive or negative reactions of the audience.

Practice Question

Alan—

I just wanted to drop you a quick note to let you know I'll be out of the office for the next two weeks. Elizabeth and I are finally taking that trip to France we've been talking about for years. It's a bit of a last-minute decision, but since we had the vacation time available, we figured it was now or never.

Anyway, my team's been briefed on the upcoming meeting, so they should be able to handle the presentation without any hiccups. If you have any questions or concerns, you can direct them to Joanie, who'll be handling my responsibilities while I'm out.

Let me know if you want any special treats. I don't know if you can take chocolate and cheese on the plane, but I'm going to try!

Best regards, Michael

14) Which word BEST describes the relationship between the author and Alan?
   A. familial
   B. formal
   C. friendly
   D. strained
   E. intimate

15) Which phrase BEST captures the author's purpose?
   A. to ask Alan if he wants any special treats from France
   B. to brag to Alan about his upcoming vacation
   C. to inform Alan that he will be out of the office
   D. to help Alan prepare for the upcoming meeting
   E. to introduce Alan to Joanie

Meaning of Words and Phrases

Some questions on the exam may ask about the definitions or intended meanings of words within passages. Even if some of these words are new, there are tricks readers can use to figure out what they mean.

Context Clues

Vocabulary-in-context questions ask about the meaning of specific words in the passage. The questions will ask which answer choice is most similar in meaning to the specified word, or which answer choice could be substituted for that word in the passage.

The passage itself can help clarify the meaning of unfamiliar words. Often, identifying the tone or main idea of the passage can help eliminate answer choices. For example, if the tone of the passage is generally positive, try eliminating the answer choices with a negative connotation. Or, if the passage is about a particular occupation, rule out words unrelated to that topic.

Passages may also provide specific **context clues** that can help determine the meaning of a word. One type of context clue is a **definition**, or **description**, **clue**. These are also known as **restatement clues**. The definition is often set apart from the rest of the sentence by a comma, parentheses, or a colon.

Sometimes authors use a difficult word, then include "that is" or "which is" to signal that they are giving a definition. An author also may use a synonym or restate the idea in more familiar words:

> Teachers often prefer teaching students with intrinsic motivation; these students have an internal desire to learn.

The meaning of "intrinsic" is restated as "internal."

Similarly, authors may include an **example clue**, using an example phrase that clarifies the meaning of the word:

> Carly found that yoga was efficacious for the cramping in her leg; the morning after yoga practice, her leg pain was gone.

"Efficacious," which means "effective," is explained with an example showing that yoga resolved the cramping in Carly's leg.

Another commonly used context clue is the **contrast**, or **antonym**, **clue**. In this case, authors indicate that the unfamiliar word is the opposite of a familiar word:

> In contrast to intrinsic motivation, extrinsic motivation is contingent on teachers offering rewards that are appealing.

The phrase "in contrast" tells the reader that "extrinsic" is the opposite of "intrinsic."

Positive/negative clues indicate whether a word has a positive or negative meaning:

> The film was lauded by critics as stunning and was nominated for several awards.

The positive descriptions "stunning" and "nominated for several awards" suggest that "lauded" has a positive meaning.

Practice Question

16) Based on context clues, which word is closest in meaning to "incentivize" as used in the following sentence?

One challenge of teaching is finding ways to incentivize, or to motivate, learning.
- A. encourage
- B. determine
- C. challenge
- D. improve
- E. dissuade

17) Based on context clues, which word is closest in meaning to "apprehensive" as used in the following sentence?

If an extrinsic reward is extremely desirable, a student may become so apprehensive he or she cannot focus. The student may experience such intense pressure to perform that the reward undermines its intent.

- A. uncertain
- B. distracted
- C. anxious
- D. forgetful
- E. resentful

Word Structure

In addition to the context of a sentence or passage, an unfamiliar word itself can give the reader clues about its meaning. Each word has separate pieces that determine meaning. The most familiar of these pieces are word roots, prefixes, and suffixes.

Word roots are the bases from which many words take their form and meaning. The most common word roots are Greek and Latin, and a broad knowledge of these roots can greatly improve a reader's ability to determine the meaning of words in context. The root of a word does not always point to the word's exact meaning, but combined with an understanding of the word's place in a sentence and the context of a passage, it will often be enough to answer a question about meaning or relationships.

Table 1.1. Common Word Roots

Root	Meaning	Examples
alter	other	alternate, alter ego
ambi	both	ambidextrous
ami, amic	love	amiable
amphi	both ends, all sides	amphibian
anthrop	man, human, humanity	misanthrope, anthropologist
apert	open	aperture
aqua	water	aqueduct, aquarium
aud	to hear	audience
auto	self	autobiography
bell	war	belligerent, bellicose
bene	good	benevolent
bio	life	biology
ced	yield, go	secede, intercede

Table 1.1. Common Word Roots

Root	Meaning	Examples
cent	one hundred	century
chron	time	chronological
circum	around	circumference
contra, counter	against	contradict
crac, crat	rule, ruler	autocrat, bureaucrat
crypt	hidden	cryptogram, cryptic
curr, curs, cours	to run	precursory
dict	to say	dictator, dictation
dyna	power	dynamic
dys	bad, hard, unlucky	dysfunctional
equ	equal, even	equanimity
fac	to make, to do	factory
form	shape	reform, conform
fort	strength	fortitude
fract	to break	fracture
grad, gress	step	progression
gram	thing written	epigram
graph	writing	graphic
hetero	different	heterogeneous
homo	same	homogenous
hypo	below, beneath	hypothermia
iso	identical	isometric
ject	throw	projection
logy	study of	biology
luc	light	elucidate
mal	bad	malevolent
meta, met	behind, between	metacognition
meter, metr	measure	thermometer

1. Reading Skills

Table 1.1. Common Word Roots

Root	Meaning	Examples
micro	small	microbe
mis, miso	hate	misanthrope
mit	to send	transmit
mono	one	monologue
morph	form, shape	morphology
mort	death	mortal
multi	many	multiple
phil	love	philanthropist
port	carry	transportation
pseudo	false	pseudonym
psycho	soul, spirit	psychic
rupt	to break	disruption
scope	viewing instrument	microscope
scrib, scribe	to write	inscription
sect, sec	to cut	section
sequ, secu	follow	consecutive
soph	wisdom, knowledge	philosophy
spect	to look	spectator
struct	to build	restructure
tele	far off	telephone
terr	earth	terrestrial
therm	heat	thermal
vent, vene	to come	convene
vert	turn	vertigo
voc	voice, call	vocalize, evocative

In addition to understanding the base of a word, readers should recognize common affixes that change the meaning of words and show their relationships to other words. **Prefixes** are added to the beginning of words and can change their meaning, sometimes to an opposite meaning.

Table 1.2. Common Prefixes

Prefix	Meaning	Examples
a, an	without, not	anachronism, anhydrous
ab, abs, a	apart, away, from	abscission, abnormal
ad	toward	adhere
agere	act	agent
amphi, ambi	round, both sides	ambivalent
ante	before	antedate, anterior
anti	against	antipathy
archos	leader, first, chief	oligarchy
bene	well, favorable	benevolent, beneficent
bi	two	binary, bivalve
caco	bad	cacophony
circum	around	circumnavigate
corpus	body	corporeal
credo	belief	credible
demos	people	demographic
di	two, double	dimorphism, diatomic
dia	across, through	dialectic
dis	not, apart	disenfranchise
dyna	be able	dynamo, dynasty
ego	I, self	egomaniac, egocentric
epi	upon, over	epigram, epiphyte
ex	out	extraneous, extemporaneous
geo	earth	geocentric, geomancy
ideo	idea	ideology, ideation
ig, im	not	ignoble, immoral
in	in	induction, indigenous
inter	between	interstellar
lexis	word	lexicography
liber	free, book	liberal

Table 1.2. Common Prefixes

Prefix	Meaning	Examples
locus	place	locality
macro	large	macrophage
micro	small	micron
mono	one, single	monocle, monovalent
mortis	death	moribund
olig	few	oligarchy
peri	around	peripatetic, perineum
poly	many	polygamy
pre	before	prescient
solus	alone	solitary
subter	under, secret	subterfuge
un	not	unsafe
utilis	useful	utilitarian

Suffixes are added to the end of words. They generally point out a word's relationship to other words in a sentence. Suffixes **might** change a part of speech or indicate if a word is plural or related to a plural.

Table 1.3. Common Suffixes

Suffix	Meaning	Examples
able, ible	able, capable	visible
age	act of, state of, result of	wreckage
al	relating to	gradual
algia	pain	myalgia
an, ian	native of, relating to	riparian
ance, ancy	action, process, state	defiance
ary, ery, ory	relating to, quality, place	aviary
cian	processing a specific skill or art	physician
cule, ling	very small	sapling, animalcule
cy	action, function	normalcy
dom	quality, realm	wisdom

1. Reading Skills

Table 1.3. Common Suffixes

Suffix	Meaning	Examples
ee	one who receives the action	nominee
en	made of, to make	silken
ence, ency	action, state of, quality	urgency
er, or	one who, that which	professor
escent	in the process of	adolescent, senescence
esis, osis	action, process, condition	genesis, neurosis
et, ette	small one, group	baronet, lorgnette
fic	making, causing	specific
ful	full of	frightful
hood	order, condition, quality	adulthood
ice	condition, state, quality	malice
id, ide	connected with, belonging to	bromide
ile	relating to, suited for, capable of	puerile, juvenile
ine	nature of	feminine
ion, sion, tion	act, result, state of	contagion
ish	origin, nature, resembling	impish
ism	system, manner, condition, characteristic	capitalism
ist	one who, that which	artist, flautist
ite	nature of, quality of, mineral product	graphite
ity, ty	state of, quality	captivity
ive	causing, making	exhaustive
ize, ise	make	idolize, bowdlerize
ment	act of, state of, result	containment
nomy	law	autonomy, taxonomy
oid	resembling	asteroid, anthropoid
some	like, apt, tending to	gruesome
strat	cover	strata

Table 1.3. Common Suffixes		
Suffix	**Meaning**	**Examples**
tude	state of, condition of	aptitude
um	forms single nouns	spectrum
ure	state of, act, process, rank	rupture, rapture
ward	in the direction of	backward
y	inclined to, tend to	faulty

Practice Question

In December of 1945, Germany launched its last major offensive campaign of World War II, pushing through the dense forests of the Ardennes region of Belgium, France, and Luxembourg. The attack, designed to block the Allies from the Belgian port of Antwerp and to split their lines, caught the Allied forces by surprise. Due to troop positioning, the Americans bore the brunt of the attack, incurring 100,000 deaths, the highest number of casualties of any battle during the war. However, after a month of grueling fighting in the bitter cold, a lack of fuel and a masterful American military strategy resulted in an Allied victory that sealed Germany's fate.

18) In the last sentence, the word "grueling" MOST nearly means
   A. exhausting.
   B. secretive.
   C. costly.
   D. intermittent.
   E. ineffective.

The Bastille, Paris's famous historic prison, was originally built in 1370 as a fortification, called a **bastide** in Old French, to protect the city from English invasion during the Hundred Years' War. It rose 100 feet into the air, had eight towers, and was surrounded by a moat more than eighty feet wide. In the seventeenth century, the government converted the fortress into an elite prison for upper-class felons, political disruptors, and spies. Residents of the Bastille arrived by direct order of the king and usually were left there to languish without a trial.

19) In the first sentence, the word "fortification" MOST nearly means
   A. royal castle.
   B. national symbol.
   C. seat of government.
   D. defensive structure.
   E. secret retreat.

Figurative Language

A figure of speech is a word or phrase with a meaning separate from its literal meaning. Figurative language suggests meaning by pointing to something else. When Shakespeare says, "All the world's a stage, and all the men and women merely players," he is speaking of the world as if it were a stage.

Since the world is not literally a stage, the reader has to ask how the world is a stage and what Shakespeare is implying about the world.

Figurative language extends the meaning of words by giving readers a new way to view a subject. Thinking of the world as a stage on which people are performing is a new way of thinking about life. After reading Shakespeare's metaphor, people may reflect on how often they play a role or act a part. They may wonder when their behavior is genuine, whether they are too worried about others evaluating their performance, and so on. Figurative language—such as metaphors and similes—generates thought after thought. With just a few words, it engages the reader's imagination and adds emphasis to different aspects of the text's subject.

> **HELPFUL HINT**
>
> Aristotle claimed that "the greatest thing by far is to have a command of metaphor. This alone cannot be imparted by another; it is the mark of genius, for to make good metaphors implies an eye for resemblances." The resemblance between two unlike things enables understanding of the ideas suggested by metaphoric language.

A **metaphor** is a figure of speech that expresses an unfamiliar *topic* in terms of a familiar *vehicle*. The familiar vehicle helps the reader understand an unfamiliar topic. Readers reflect on the similarities between the topic and the vehicle and form a new idea about the topic. For example, if a person refers to an issue as "the elephant in the room," the topic is the issue, and "the elephant in the room" is the vehicle. In this example, the vehicle shows that the issue is undeniable or overwhelming.

In **personification**, an object is anthropomorphized—receives a human attribute. In the sentence "The earth swallowed him whole," "earth" is personified: it carries out a human action. Personification may also represent an abstract quality. For instance, a timid individual may be the "personification of cowardice."

A **simile** directly points to similarities between two things. The author uses a familiar vehicle to express an idea about the topic. For example, in his poem "The Rime of the Ancient Mariner," Samuel Taylor Coleridge describes his ship as "Idle as a painted ship upon a painted ocean." Since most readers have seen a painting of a ship, Coleridge uses this knowledge to convey that the ship was completely motionless. Like a simile, an **analogy** is a correspondence between two things; it shows a partial similarity.

Practice Question

Alfie closed his eyes and took several deep breaths. He was trying to ignore the sounds of the crowd, but even he had to admit that it was hard not to notice the tension in the stadium. He could feel 50,000 sets of eyes burning through his skin—this crowd expected perfection from him. He took another breath and opened his eyes, setting his sights on the soccer ball resting peacefully in the grass. One shot, just one last shot, between his team and the championship. He didn't look up at the goalie, who was jumping nervously on the goal line just a few yards away. Afterward, he would swear he didn't remember anything between the referee's whistle and the thunderous roar of the crowd.

20) Which sentence BEST describes the meaning of the phrase "He could feel 50,000 sets of eyes burning through his skin"?
  - A. The 50,000 people in the stadium were trying to hurt Alfie.
  - B. Alfie felt uncomfortable and exposed in front of so many people.
  - C. Alfie felt immense pressure from the 50,000 people watching him.
  - D. The people in the stadium are warning Alfie that the field is on fire.
  - E. The crowd was angry at Alfie.

Comparing Passages

Some of the questions in the CBEST Reading exam ask test takers to compare texts with similar themes or topics. Test takers will have to identify the similarities and differences in main ideas, styles, supporting details, and text structures. Previewing the questions and noting similarities and differences in texts while reading will be helpful.

The following passages discuss cicadas, a common insect in the United States.

Readers should keep in mind the following questions:

  - What central idea about cicadas is being expressed in the passages?

  - How does the tone of Passage A differ from that of Passage B?

Practice Question

Passage A

Cicadas are familiar to many Americans due to their buzzing, clicking song. In the eastern part of the United States, during the summer the air echoes with the humming of the cicada, an oval-shaped insect that can reach up to 2.5 inches in length. Cicadas are harmless: they do not sting or bite humans. They emerge from the ground in the summer to mate. Cicadas live underground as juveniles, or nymphs, and shed their skin, or exoskeletons, to take on their adult form. Cicadas are found in Texas, the southeastern United States, the mid-Atlantic, and range up through New York State and southern New England. They also inhabit the Midwest.

Passage B

The sounds of summer in the eastern United States feature the lazy buzzing of the cicada. Did you know that there are actually two kinds of cicadas? Some breeds emerge every year to hum away through the hot summer days. Others spend thirteen or even seventeen years underground as babies, or nymphs, only coming out into the light after all that time to mate and die! Cicadas may look a little scary, but don't worry: they are not a threat to humans. Even though they can get quite large for insects, growing to up to 2.5 inches, they eat twigs and liquid from plants. Adult cicadas do not eat at all. They only live for a short time to mate.

21) What argument do both sources share about cicadas?
    A. Cicadas live throughout the United States.
    B. The sound of cicadas is familiar to Americans in the eastern United States.
    C. Cicadas are dangerous insects because they are poisonous.
    D. American crops are plagued by cicadas every summer.
    E. The western states are home to cicadas that emerge every seventeen years.

22) What is the main difference between the passages?
    A. Passage A discusses the geographic range of cicadas. Passage B discusses what they eat.
    B. Passage A talks about the cicadas that emerge every seventeen years. Passage B does not.
    C. Passage A has a more formal tone, while Passage B has a more informal tone.
    D. Passage A argues that cicadas are important in the environment. Passage B warns of their harm.
    E. Passage A was written by a scientist. Passage B was written by a student.

Indexes and Tables of Contents

An index is an alphabetical list of topics, and their associated page numbers, covered in a text. A table of contents is an outline of a text that includes topics, organized by page number. Both of these can be used to look up information, but they have slightly different purposes. An index helps the reader determine where in the text to find specific details. A table of contents shows the reader the general arrangement of the text.

> **QUICK REVIEW**
>
> When would it be appropriate to use an index but NOT a table of contents?

Practice Question

23) According to the index below, where might the reader find information about the nursing code of ethics?

Nursing	189-296
Certification	192-236
Code of ethics	237-291
Procedures	292-296

    A. pages 189 – 236
    B. pages 189 – 296
    C. pages 192 – 236
    D. pages 237 – 291
    E. pages 292 – 296

24) A student has been assigned a set of homework questions from page 125. What topic will the questions cover?

Table of Contents

Chapter 1: Pre-Algebra	5
Chapter 2: Algebra	35
Chapter 3: Geometry	115
Chapter 4: Trigonometry	175

- A. Pre-Algebra
- B. Algebra
- C. Geometry
- D. Trigonometry
- E. Calculus

Text Features

Text features are stylistic elements used to clarify, add meaning, or differentiate. Examples of text features include bold, italicized, or underlined fonts, and bulleted or numbered lists.

Bold fonts are generally used for emphasis. Italics should be used for titles of longer works, such as novels, movies, books, magazines, and plays. They are also used to denote a foreign word or phrase. Note that italicized fonts and underlined fonts serve similar purposes and are often used interchangeably. Underlining is more commonly used in handwritten documents.

Practice Question

25) Which of the following sentences properly uses italics?
- A. We enjoyed our vacation in Sacramento, California.
- B. Adam ate two plates of pasta with meatballs.
- C. Angela's favorite book is The Art of War.
- D. The traffic on Main Street is terrible during rush hour.
- E. I must work over Memorial Day weekend.

Answer Key

1) E: The author writes, "the allied tribes...decisively defeated their US foes."

2) B: The author writes, "From this, scientists learned that different types of memory are handled by different parts of the brain."

3) B: This is the first sentence of the passage and introduces the topic: limitations on government provided by the US Constitution.

4) A: This is the last sentence of the passage and summarizes the passage's content.

5) C: The author writes, "First...it recorded data on Titan's curious methane lakes, gathering information about potential seasons on the planet-sized moon."

6) A: A company that profits from private tutoring might be biased in a study on the effects of private tutoring in schools.

7) B: The writer uses the first person, showing his or her opinion, to recommend a French press as the best way to brew coffee.

8) B: The author describes the level of destruction in detail, suggesting it had a significant negative impact on the Confederacy.

9) D: The author writes that "the reason for the cisco's reemergence is even more unlikely. The cisco have an invasive species, quagga mussels, to thank for their return."

10) C: The author explains why the gun was created, how it functions, and how it was first used.

11) A: The passage explains how a baby's senses develop and allow him or her to interact with the world.

12) D: The author draws a contrast between the way vision and the other senses develop in babies.

13) B: The purpose of the passage is to explain what an idealist believes in. The author does not offer any opinions or try to persuade readers about the importance of certain values.

14) C: The author and Alan have a friendly relationship, as evidenced by the author's casual tone and his offer to bring Alan a gift from his vacation.

15) C: The author is writing to tell Alan that he will be out of the office. The details about his trip and the meeting support this idea.

16) A: The word "incentivize" is defined immediately with the synonym "motivate," or to encourage.

17) C: The reader can use context clues to determine that the pressure to perform is making the student anxious.

18) A: The context implies that the fighting was intense and tiring.

19) D: The author writes that the Bastille was originally built "to protect the city from English invasion during the Hundred Years' War."

20) C: The metaphor implies that Alfie felt pressure to perform well from the people watching him. There is no indication that he is threatened physically.

21) B: Both passages mention the song of cicadas throughout the eastern United States. Passage A states, "In the eastern part of the United States, during the summer the air echoes with the humming of the cicada." According to Passage B, "The sounds of summer in the eastern United States feature the lazy buzzing of the cicada."

22) C: Passage A has a more formal tone, and Passage B uses a more informal tone with contractions and direct address: "Did you know that there are actually two kinds of cicadas?... Cicadas may look a little scary, but don't worry..."

23) D: According to the index, this information can be found between pages 237 and 291.

24) C: According to the table of contents, page 125 is in Chapter 3: Geometry.

25) C: The sentence in choice C italicizes the title of a longer work and is therefore correct. Italics are not used for names of cities (choice A), foods (choice B), streets (choice D), or holidays (choice E).

2. Mathematics

Estimation, Measurement, and Statistical Principles

Units

The United States uses **customary units**, sometimes called standard units. Most countries use the **metric system**, which uses a different set of units.

Dimension	Customary Units	Metric Units	Converting Between Customary Units	Converting Between Customary and Metric Units
length	inch (in) foot (ft) yard (yd) mile (mi)	meter (m)	$12\ inches\ =\ 1\ foot$ $3\ feet\ =\ 1\ yard$ $5280\ feet\ =\ 1\ mile$	$1\ in\ =\ 2.54\ cm$ $1\ ft\ =\ 0.3\ m$ $1\ yd\ =\ 0.914\ m$ $1\ mi\ =\ 1.61\ km$
mass	ounce (oz) pound (lb)	gram (g)	$16\ ounces\ =\ 1\ pound$ $2000\ pounds\ =\ 1\ ton$	$1\ oz\ =\ 28.35\ g$ $1\ lb\ =\ 0.454\ kg$
volume	fluid ounce (fl oz) cup (c) pint (pt) quart (qt) gallon (gal)	liter (L)	$8\ fluid\ ounces\ =\ 1\ cup$ $2\ cups\ =\ 1\ pint$ $2\ pints\ =\ 1\ quart$ $4\ quarts\ =\ 1\ gallon$	$1\ gal\ =\ 3.785\ L$

Table 2.1. US Customary Units

The metric system also uses a set of prefixes to make it easier to express very large and very small measurements. The prefixes are added to the unit.

$$1000\ meters\ =\ 1\ kilometer$$

$$1000\ m\ =\ 1\ km$$

Table 2.2. Metric Prefixes

Prefix	Symbol	Multiplication Factor
tera	T	1,000,000,000,000
giga	G	1,000,000,000
mega	M	1,000,000
kilo	k	1,000
hecto	h	100
deca	da	10
base unit		
deci	d	0.1
centi	c	0.01
milli	m	0.001
micro	μ	0.0000001
nano	n	0.0000000001
pico	p	0.0000000000001

Units can be converted within the customary system and between the two systems using dimensional analysis. Start with the original unit and multiply by the conversion factor (written as a fraction like $\frac{1000\ m}{1\ km}$) to get the new unit. Note that units that appear on the top and bottom cancel out.

$$\frac{120\ in}{} \times \frac{1\ ft}{12\ in} = 10\ ft$$

$$6\frac{m}{s} = \frac{6\ m}{1\ s} \times \frac{1ft}{0.3m} = \frac{6ft}{0.3s} = 20\frac{ft}{s}$$

A similar strategy can be used to solve problems that involve a rate, such as meters per second or miles per hour. These problems will ask for quantities like distance or time. Place the standalone value on the left, and multiply by the rate.

How long will it take a car traveling 60 miles per hour to travel 300 miles?

$$\frac{300\ miles}{} \times \frac{1\ hour}{60\ miles} = 5\ hours$$

Practice Question

1) Which of the following is an appropriate unit for measuring the height of an adult?
   A. pound
   B. kilometer
   C. liter
   D. mile
   E. meter

2) A 10,000-gallon pool is being filled at a rate of x gallons per minute. Which of the following expressions describes the length of time in minutes it will take for the pool to be full?
   A. $10,000x$
   B. $\frac{10,000}{x}$
   C. $10,000 + x$
   D. $\frac{10,000 + x}{x}$
   E. $x - 10,000$

Lines and Angles

Geometric figures are shapes composed of points, lines, or planes. A **point** is simply a location in space; it does not have any dimensional properties such as length, area, or volume. Points are written as a single capital letter, such as *A* or *Q*.

A collection of points that extends infinitely in both directions is a *line*, and one that extends infinitely in only one direction is a *ray*. A section of a line with a beginning and end is a *line segment*. A line segment is described by the beginning and end point, such as *AQ*. Lines, rays, and line segments are examples of **one-dimensional objects** because they can only be measured in one dimension (length).

> **HELPFUL HINT**
>
> Two lines that form right angles are **perpendicular**. Lines that do not intersect are described as **parallel**.

Lines, rays, and line segments can intersect to create angles, which are measured in degrees or radians. Angles are classified based on the number of degrees they contain.

- Angles between 0 and 90 degrees are **acute**.
- Angles between 90 and 180 degrees are **obtuse**.
- An angle of exactly 90 degrees is a **right angle**.

Two angles with measurements that add up to 90 degrees are **complementary**, and two angles with measurements that add up to 180 degrees are **supplementary**. Two adjacent (touching) angles are called a **linear pair**, and they are supplementary.

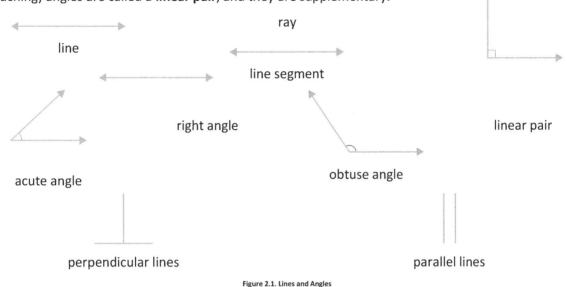

Figure 2.1. Lines and Angles

Practice Question

3) Mrs. Cortez is working with her students on comparing angles. A worksheet includes a picture of the following angle and asks students to draw a larger angle.

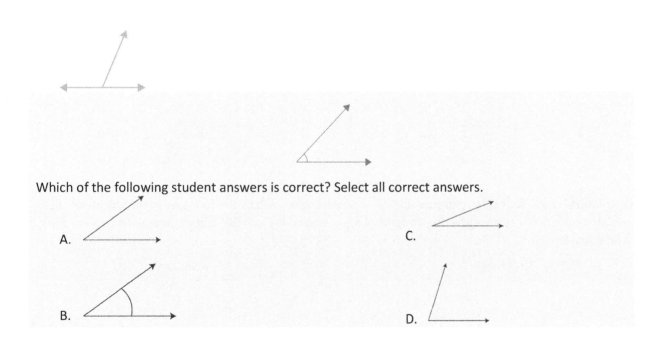

Which of the following student answers is correct? Select all correct answers.

Properties of Two-Dimensional Shapes

Two-dimensional objects can be measured in two dimensions (length and width). A **plane** is a two-dimensional object that extends infinitely in both dimensions. **Polygons** are two-dimensional shapes, such as triangles and squares, that have three or more straight sides. **Regular polygons** are polygons with sides that are all the same length.

> **HELPFUL HINT**
>
> Because all the points on a circle are equidistant from the center, all the circle's radii have the same length.

A **circle** is the set of all the points in a plane that are the same distance from a fixed point (called the **center**). The distance from the center to any point on the circle is the **radius** of the circle. The **diameter** is the largest measurement across a circle. It passes through the circle's center, extending from one side of the circle to the other. The measure of the diameter is twice the measure of the radius.

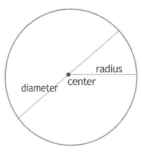

Figure 2.2. Parts of a Circle

Triangles have three sides and three interior angles that always sum to 180°. A **scalene triangle** has no equal sides or angles. An **isosceles triangle** has two equal sides and two equal angles (often called base angles). In an **equilateral triangle**, all three sides are equal as are all three angles. Moreover, because the sum of the angles of a triangle is always 180°, each angle of an equilateral triangle must be 60°.

Scalene   **Isosceles**   **Equilateral**

Figure 2.3. Types of Triangles

Quadrilaterals have four sides and four angles. In a **rectangle**, each of the four angles measures 90° and there are two pairs of sides with equal lengths. A square also has four 90° angles, and all four of its sides are an equal length.

Rectangle   Square

Figure 2.4. Quadrilaterals

The size of the surface of a two-dimensional object is its **area**. The distance around a two-dimensional figure is its **perimeter**, which can be found by adding the lengths of all the sides.

Table 2.3. Area and Perimeter of Basic Shapes			
Shape	Area	Perimeter	Variables
Triangle	$A = \dfrac{1}{2}bh$	$P = s^1 + s^2 + s^3$	$b = base$ $h = height$
Square	$A = s^2$	$P = 4s$	$s = side$
Rectangle	$A = l \times w$	$P = 2l + 2w$	$l = length$ $w = width$
Circle	$A = \pi r^2$	$C = 2\pi r$	$r = radius$ $C = circumference$

Practice Question

4) Which of the following expressions describes the area of the triangle below?

A. $x + y + z$

B. $\dfrac{xy}{2}$

C. xyz

D. $\dfrac{xyz}{2}$

E. $2xy$

5) The figure below shows a square with four equal cutouts on each corner. What is the area of the resulting shape?

A. $6\ mm^2$
B. $16\ mm^2$
C. $64\ mm^2$
D. $128\ mm^2$
E. $144\ mm^2$

Properties of Three-Dimensional Shapes

Three-dimensional objects, such as cubes, can be measured in three dimensions (length, width, height). Three-dimensional objects are also called **solids**, and the shape of a flattened solid is called a **net**.

The **surface area** (SA) of a three-dimensional object can be figured by adding the areas of all the sides. Surface area is measured in square units (e.g., m^2 or ft^2). **Volume** (V) is the amount of space that a three-dimensional object takes up.

Volume is measured in cubic units (e.g., ft^3 or mm^3).

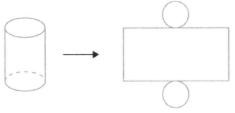

Figure 2.5. Net of a Cylinder

A **rectangular solid** has six rectangular sides.

A **cube** is a type of rectangular solid in which all the sides are squares. Every rectangular solid has a width (*w*), a length (*l*), and a height (*h*). Its surface area is the sum of the area of each rectangle, and its volume is found by multiplying the width, length, and height.

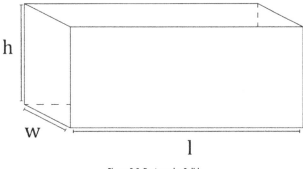

Figure 2.6. Rectangular Solid

$$SA = 2lw + 2hw + 2hl$$

$$V = wlh$$

Practice Question

6) A rectangular tank with a width of 3 meters and a length of 5 meters is filled with 30 cubic meters of water. What will be the height of the water in meters?

Measures of Central Tendency

Measures of central tendency help identify the center, or most typical, value within a data set. There are three such central tendencies that describe the "center" of the data in different ways. The **mean** (μ) is the arithmetic average and is found by dividing the sum of all measurements by the number of measurements.

$$\mu = \frac{x_1 + x_2 + \cdots x_N}{N}$$

Find the mean of the following data set: {75, 62, 78, 92, 83, 90}

$$\frac{75 + 62 + 78 + 92 + 83 + 90}{6} = \frac{480}{6} = 80$$

The **median** divides a set into two equal halves. To calculate the median, place the data set in ascending order. The median is the measurement right in the middle of an odd set of measurements or the average of the two middle numbers in an even data set.

Find the median of the following data set:

$$\{2, 15, 16, 8, 21, 13, 4\}$$

Place the data in ascending order:

$$\{2, 4, 8, 13, 15, 16, 21\}$$

The median is the value in the middle:

$$13$$

Find the median of the following data set:

$$\{75, 62, 78, 92, 83, 91\}$$

Place the data in ascending order:

$$\{62, 75, 78, 83, 91, 92\}$$

Find the average of the two middle values:

$$\frac{(78 + 83)}{2} = 80.5$$

Outliers are values in a data set that are much larger or smaller than the other values in the set. Outliers can skew the mean, making it higher or lower than most of the values. The median is not affected by outliers, so it is a better measure of central tendency when outliers are present.

For the set {3, 5, 10, 12, 65}:

$$mean = \frac{3 + 5 + 10 + 12 + 65}{5} = 19$$

$$median = 10$$

The outlier (65) drags the mean much higher than the median.

The **mode** is simply the measurement that occurs most often. There can be one, several, or no modes in a data set.

Practice Question

7) A student has an average of 81 on four equally weighted tests she has taken in her statistics class. She wants to determine what grade she must receive on her fifth test so that her mean is 83. What grade must she receive on her fifth test?
    A. 81
    B. 83
    C. 85
    D. 89
    E. 91

Measures of Dispersion

The values in a data set can be very close together (close to the mean) or very spread out. This is called the **spread** or **dispersion** of the data. There are a few **measures of dispersion** that quantify the spread within a data set. **Range** is the difference between the largest and smallest data points in a set:

$$R = largest\ data\ point - smallest\ data\ point$$

Notice range depends on only two data points, the two extremes. Sometimes these data points are outliers; regardless, for a large data set, relying on only two data points is not an exact tool. To better understand the data set, calculate **quartiles**, which divide data sets into four equally sized groups. To calculate quartiles:

1. Arrange the data in ascending order.

2. Find the set's median (also called quartile 2 or Q2).

3. Find the median of the lower half of the data, called quartile 1 (Q1).

4. Find the median of the upper half of the data, called quartile 3 (Q3).

The interquartile range (IQR) provides a more reliable range that is not as affected by extremes. IQR is the difference between the third quartile data point and the first quartile data point:

$$IQR = Q_3 - Q_1$$

Practice Question

8) The table below shows the number of customers that came into a restaurant each day of the week. What is the range of the data set?

Day of the Week	Number of Customers
Monday	72
Tuesday	89
Wednesday	125
Thursday	212
Friday	350
Saturday	418
Sunday	262

Probability

Probability (*P*) is the likelihood of one or a certain number of specific events occurring. The probability of a single event occurring is the number of outcomes in which that event occurs (called **favorable events**) divided by the number of items in the **Example space** (total possible outcomes):

$$P \ (an \ event) \ = \ \frac{number \ of \ favorable \ outcomes}{total \ number \ of \ possible \ outcomes}$$

The probability of any event occurring will always be a fraction or decimal between 0 and 1. It may also be expressed as a percent. The probability of an event not occurring is referred to as that event's **complement**. The sum of an event's probability and the probability of that event's complement will always be 1.

> **HELPFUL HINT**
>
> An event with 0 (or 0%) probability will never occur, and an event with a probability of 1 (or 100%) is certain to occur.

If events are **dependent events**, the probability of one occurring changes the probability of the other event occurring. If events are **independent events**, the probability of one occurring does not affect the probability of the other event occurring. Rolling a die multiple times is independent: getting one number does not change the probability of getting any particular number on the next roll.

The probability of two *independent events* occurring is the product of the two events' probabilities:

$$P(A \ and \ B) \ = \ P(A) \ \times \ P(B)$$

Practice Question

9) In 2018 in the United States, 3.2 million teachers were employed by public schools, and 0.5 million teachers were employed by private schools. What is the probability that a US teacher selected at random works at a private school?
- A. 5%
- B. 14%
- C. 16%
- D. 72%
- E. 86%

Estimation and Rounding

Rounding is used to make numbers easier to work with. The process makes numbers less accurate, but makes operations and mental math easier. Rounding is performed to a specific place value, such as the thousands or tenths place.

To round a number, first identify the digit in the specified place (such as the tens or hundreds). Then look at the digit one place to the right. If that digit is four or less, keep the digit in the specified place the same. If that digit is five or more, add 1 to the digit in the specified place. All the digits to the right of the specified place become zeros.

rounded to the hundreds place:

$$5,372 \rightarrow 5,400$$

rounded to the tens place:

$$5,372 \rightarrow 5,370$$

rounded to the tenths place:

$$11.635 \rightarrow 11.600$$

rounded to the hundredths place:

$$11.635 \rightarrow 11.640$$

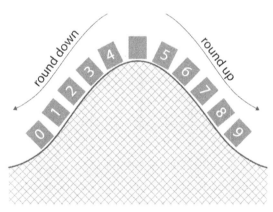

Figure 2.7. Rounding

Estimation is when numbers are rounded and then an operation is performed. This process can be used when working with large numbers to find a close, but not exact, answer.

Practice Question

10) What is 498,235 rounded to the nearest thousands?
- A. 497,000
- B. 498,000
- C. 498,200
- D. 499,000
- E. 500,000

11) Which of the following is closest in value to 129,113 + 34,602?
   A. 162,000
   B. 163,000
   C. 164,000
   D. 165,000
   E. 166,000

Computation and Problem Solving

Types of Numbers

Numbers can be classified into various groups based on their properties.

- **Natural numbers** are the numbers used to count objects: 1, 2, 3, 4, ...

- **Whole numbers** include all the natural numbers and 0.

- **Integers** include 0, the natural numbers (also called positive numbers), and their opposites, the negative integers (−1, −2, −3, ...).

- **Positive numbers** are greater than 0, and **negative numbers** are less than 0. Both positive and negative numbers can be shown on a number line.

Figure 2.8. Number Line

- **Rational numbers** are defined as any number that can be written as a fraction (a part over a whole, such as $\frac{3}{4}$). Rational numbers include all integers and the fractional values between them.

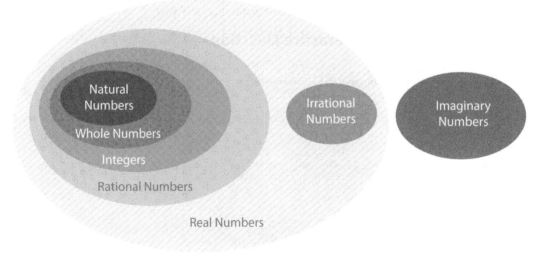

Figure 2.9. Types of Numbers

Practice Question

12) A student claims that "all integers are also whole numbers." Which of the following numbers is a counterexample to the student's claim?

    A. −5
    B. 0
    C. $\frac{2}{3}$
    D. 1
    E. 100

Basic Operations

The four basic arithmetic operations are addition, subtraction, multiplication, and division.

Add (+) to combine two quantities. The quantities being added are called the **addends**. **Subtract** (−) to find the difference of two quantities. Subtraction is the opposite of addition.

> **HELPFUL HINT**
>
> The absolute value of a number is the number without a sign.

- If the numbers have the same sign, add their absolute values and give the answer the same sign.

$$-2 + (-7) = -9$$

- If the numbers have different signs, subtract their absolute values. Then give the answer the sign of the number with the largest absolute value.

$$4 + (-9) = -5$$

- To subtract two numbers, change the sign of the second number and add.

$$6 - 11 = 6 + (-11) = -5$$

$$12 - (-10) = 12 + 10 = 22$$

Addition can also be visualized on a number line. Start with the first addend, then move to the right or left depending on the sign of the second addend.

Multiply (×) to add a quantity multiple times (e.g., $6 \times 3 = 6 + 6 + 6 = 18$). The numbers being multiplied together are called **factors**. **Divide** (÷) to find out how many times one quantity goes into another. Division is the opposite of multiplication.

> **HELPFUL HINT**
>
> The remainder is what is left over when one number does not divide evenly into another. For example, when 13 is divided 4($13 \div 4$ or $\frac{13}{4}$), remainder of 1.

- If the signs are the same, make the answer positive.

$$-3 \times -4 = 12$$

- If the signs are different, make the answer negative.

$$-30 \div 10 = -3$$

Practice Question

13) The temperature on a cold day in January was –3°F. When the sun went down, the temperature fell 5 degrees. What was the temperature after the sun went down?
   A. –15°F
   B. –8°F
   C. 0°F
   D. 2°F
   E. 15°F

14) A case of pencils contains 24 boxes. Each box contains 110 pencils. How many pencils are in the case?
   A. 86
   B. 134
   C. 2640
   D. 5280
   E. 290,400

Order of Operations

The **order of operations** is a set of rules for simplifying expressions that include more than one operation. The rules describe the order in which operations should be performed:

   1. Parentheses—Perform operations within parentheses or other grouping symbols, such as brackets.

   2. Exponents—Simplify exponential expressions.

   3. Multiplication and division—Work multiplication and division from left to right. Multiplication does not necessarily come before division.

   4. Addition and subtraction—Work addition and subtraction from left to right. Addition does not necessarily come before subtraction.

The acronym **PEMDAS** is often used to remember the order of operations.

Practice Question

15) Which of the following is equivalent to $7 + 24 \div 8 \times (4 - 6)^2$?
   A. 1
   B. 15.5
   C. 19
   D. 40
   E. 90.25

Properties of Whole Numbers

Every whole number (except 1) is either a prime number or a composite number.

- A **prime number** is a natural number greater than 1 that can be divided evenly only by 1 and itself. For example, 7 is a prime number because it is divisible only by 1 and 7.

- A **composite number** is a natural number greater than 1 that can be evenly divided by at least one other number besides 1 and itself. For example, 6 is a composite number because it can be divided by 1, 2, 3, and 6.

Composite numbers can be broken down into **factors**: the numbers that are multiplied together to produce the composite number. Factors can be found by finding all the sets of multiples that produce the composite number. The example below shows all the factors of 54.

$$54 = 54 \times 1$$

$$54 = 27 \times 2$$

$$54 = 18 \times 3$$

$$54 = 9 \times 6$$

The factors of 54 are 1, 2, 3, 6, 9, 18, 27, and 54.

Figure 2.11 shows how the number 54 can be broken down into prime factors: $54 = 2 \times 3 \times 3 \times 3$.

Figure 2.11. Factor Tree

The **greatest common factor (GCF)** of a set of numbers, also called the **greatest common divisor**, is the greatest number (other than 1) that each number in the set is divisible by without any remainders. The GCF may be one of the numbers; for example, for the numbers 4 and 8, the GCF is 4, since 4 goes into both 4 and 8.

The **least common multiple (LCM)** of a set of numbers is the smallest number that is a multiple of all the numbers in the set. The LCM is often called the **least common denominator (LCD)**, especially when it is used to add and subtract fractions. To find the LCM of numbers, write out all the

> **HELPFUL HINT**
>
> Even numbers are multiples of 2, meaning they have 2 as a factor (2, 4, 6,...).
>
> Odd numbers have a remainder when divided by 2.

multiples and look for the smallest number that is in both lists.

6: 6, 12, 18, 24, 30

8: 8, 16, 24, 32

The least common multiple of 6 and 8 is 24.

Practice Question

16) In the Venn diagram below, circle A represents all the factors of 12 and circle B represents all the factors of 26. How many numbers are included in the shaded region?

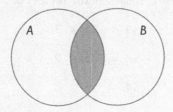

A. 0
B. 1
C. 2
D. 3
E. 4

Fractions

A **fraction** represents parts of a whole. The top number of a fraction, called the **numerator**, indicates how many equal-sized parts are present. The bottom number of a fraction, called the **denominator**, indicates how many equal-sized parts make a whole.

Fractions have several forms:

- **proper fraction:** the numerator is less than the denominator

- **improper fraction:** the numerator is greater than or equal to the denominator

- **mixed number:** the combination of a whole number and a fraction

2. Mathematics

Improper fractions can be converted to mixed numbers by dividing. (The fraction bar is also a division symbol.) The remainder becomes the new numerator.

$$\frac{9}{4} = 2\frac{1}{4}$$

To convert a mixed number to a fraction, multiply the whole number by the denominator of the fraction, and add the numerator. The result becomes the numerator of the improper fraction; the denominator remains the same.

$$3\frac{2}{5} = \frac{(3 \times 5) + 2}{5} = \frac{17}{5}$$

HELPFUL HINT

To create equivalent fractions (fractions that are equal), multiply the numerator and denominator by the same number.

Adding or subtracting fractions requires a **common denominator**. This value may be the least common denominator. However, the easiest way to find a common denominator is simply to multiply all the denominators together.

Multiply each fraction by the value needed to create a common denominator. Once all the denominators are the same, add or subtract the numerators.

$$\frac{3}{10} + \frac{2}{3} = \left(\frac{3}{3}\right)\frac{3}{10} + \left(\frac{10}{10}\right)\frac{2}{3} = \frac{9}{30} + \frac{20}{30} = \frac{29}{30}$$

$$\frac{3}{5} - \frac{1}{4} = \left(\frac{4}{4}\right)\frac{3}{5} - \left(\frac{5}{5}\right)\frac{1}{4} = \frac{12}{20} - \frac{5}{20} = \frac{7}{20}$$

A common denominator is not necessary for multiplication or division of fractions. To multiply fractions, multiply numerators and multiply denominators. Reduce the product to lowest terms.

$$\frac{5}{6} \times \frac{2}{3} = \frac{5 \times 2}{6 \times 3} = \frac{10}{18} = \frac{5}{9}$$

$$\frac{2}{3} \div \frac{1}{4} = \frac{2}{3} \times \frac{4}{1} = \frac{8}{3}$$

When multiplying and dividing mixed numbers, the mixed numbers must be converted to improper fractions.

$$2\frac{3}{7} \times \frac{1}{2} = \frac{17}{7} \times \frac{1}{2} = \frac{17}{14}$$

Practice Question

17) Carla divides her pizza into 8 equal slices and takes 1 piece. If the amount of pizza remaining is written as a fraction, the numerator will be:

    A. 0
    B. 1
    C. 7
    D. 8
    E. 9

18) A student is taking a survey of her classmates for a project. She finds that $\frac{3}{4}$ of students have a favorite book. Of the students who have a favorite book, $\frac{1}{5}$ say that *The Hunger Games* is their favorite book. What fraction of the total class says that *The Hunger Games* is their favorite book?

___

Decimals

Decimal numbers use decimal notation to express fractions with denominators that are powers of ten. Each digit to the right of the decimal point has a place value of tenths, hundredths, thousandths, and so on. For example, the fraction $\frac{319}{1000}$ written in decimal notation would be 0.319.

1,000,000	100,000	10,000	1,000	100	10	1	.	1/10	1/100
10^6	10^5	10^4	10^3	10^2	10^1	10^0	.	10^{-1}	10^{-2}
Millions	Hundred Thousands	Ten Thousands	Thousands	Hundreds	Tens	Ones	Decimal	Tenths	Hundreths

To convert a decimal number to a fraction, write the digits in the numerator and write the place value of the final digit in the denominator. Reduce to lowest terms, if necessary.

$$0.092 = \frac{92}{1000} = \frac{92 \div 4}{1000 \div 4} = \frac{23}{250}$$

To convert a fraction to a decimal, divide the numerator by the denominator.

$$\frac{5}{8} = 5 \div 8 = 0.625$$

Practice Question

19) Which digit is in the hundredths place when 1.3208 is divided by 5.2?
   A. 0
   B. 2
   C. 4
   D. 5
   E. 8

Ratios and Proportions

A **ratio** is a comparison of two quantities. For example, if a class consists of 15 women and 10 men, the ratio of women to men is 15 to 10. This ratio can also be written as 15:10 or $\frac{15}{10}$. Ratios, like fractions, can be reduced. To **reduce** a fraction or ratio, divide each number by the largest factor they share.

> **HELPFUL HINT**
>
> Cross product:
> $$\frac{a}{b} = \frac{c}{d} \rightarrow ad = bc$$

$$\frac{25}{15} = \frac{25 \div 5}{15 \div 5} = \frac{5}{3}$$

A **proportion** is a statement that two ratios are equal. For example, proportion $\frac{5}{10} = \frac{7}{14}$ is true because both ratios are equal to $\frac{1}{2}$.

Proportions have a useful quality: their cross-products are equal. For the example proportion above:

$$\frac{5}{10} = \frac{7}{14}$$

$$5(14) = 7(10)$$

$$70 = 70$$

The fact that the cross-products of proportions are equal can be used to solve proportions in which one of the values is missing. (See Algebra Equations later in this chapter.)

$$\frac{6}{13} = \frac{x}{39}$$

$$13x = 6(39)$$

$$13x = 234$$

$$x = 18$$

Practice Question

20) A company employs 30 people, 12 of whom are men. What is the ratio of women to men working at the company?

21) The dosage for a particular medication is proportional to the weight of the patient. If the dosage for a patient weighing 60 kg is 90 mg, what is the dosage for a patient weighing 80 kg?
   A.   40 mg
   B.   120 mg
   C.   160 mg
   D.   180 mg
   E.   7200 mg

Percentages

A **percent** (or percentage) means *per hundred* and is expressed with the percent symbol, %. For example, 54% means 54 out of every 100. Percentages are turned into decimals by moving the decimal point two places to the left, so 54% = 0.54. Percentages can be solved by setting up a proportion:

$$\frac{part}{whole} = \frac{\%}{100}$$

Percent change describes how much a value has increased or decreased. It is found using the formula:

$$percent\ change = \frac{new\ amount - old\ amount}{old\ amount} \times 100$$

To find the amount that a value has changed, it's often easier to use the formula given below, where percent change is given as a decimal:

$$amount\ of\ change = original\ amount \times percent\ change$$

HELPFUL HINT

Key words for percent increase: "markup," "growth," "increased." Key words for percent decrease: "marked down," "sale," "decreased."

Practice Question

22) 16 is 80% of what number?

23) A store owner buys 100 textbooks for $16 per book. If he marks up each book by 8% and sells all the books, what will his profit be?
   A. $128
   B. $160
   C. $168
   D. $1600
   E. $1728

Algebraic Expressions

An **algebraic expression** is a mathematical phrase involving both numbers and **variables**, such as x or a, that represent unknown values. Variables can be multiplied by **coefficients**, which are numbers placed in front of the variable. In the expression $2x + 3$, x is the variable, and 2 is the coefficient. The number 3 is called a constant because its value cannot vary.

A **term** is a collection of coefficients and variables multiplied together, such as $5a$ or $21xy$. The terms of algebraic expressions are separated by plus and minus signs.

Expressions are evaluated by plugging in a given value for the variable. This process has two steps:

   1. Substitute—replace the variable with the value assigned to it.

   2. Simplify—work out the expression according to the order of operations.

What is the value of $3x^2 - 4x + 1$ when $x = 5$?

Replace x with 5.

$$3x^2 - 4x + 1$$

$$3(5)^2 - 4(5) + 1 = 56$$

To add or subtract algebraic expressions, combine like terms. Like terms have the same variable (or no variable) raised to the same power. Note that variables that stand alone have a coefficient of 1.

Simplify the expression: $\left(3x^2 - 4x + 2\right) - (x^2 + 2x + 5)$

Remove the parentheses, distributing -1 to the second expression.

$$(3x^2 - 4x + 2) - (x^2 + 2x + 5)$$

$$= 3x^2 - 4x + 2 - x^2 - 2x - 5$$

Combine like terms.

$$= 3x^2 - x^2 - 4x - 2x + 2 - 5$$

$$= 2x^2 - 6x - 3$$

Practice Question

24) Which of the following is equivalent to $3x(x + 7) + 4x(2x - 6)$ for all values of x?

    A. 12

    B. $7x$

    C. $10x + 22$

    D. $11x^2 - 3x$

    E. $11x^2 - x + 1$

Algebraic Equations

An **equation** is a mathematical sentence that contains an equal sign: it states that two expressions are equal to each other. Because the two sides of the equation are equal, the same operation can be performed on both sides of the equation and it will still be true.

Solving an equation means finding the value of the variable that makes the equation true. This value can be found by performing operations so that the variable is alone on one side of the equal sign and a constant is on the other side of the equal sign.

Figure 2.14. Equations

Solve for x: $4x + 5 = 2x - 7$

Subtract $2x$ from both sides.

$$4x + 5 = 2x - 7$$

$$4x - 2x + 5 = 2x - 2x - 7$$

$$2x + 5 = -7$$

Subtract 5 from both sides.

$$2x + 5 - 5 = -7 - 5$$

$$2x = -12$$

Divide both sides by 2.

$$\frac{2x}{2} = \frac{-12}{2}$$

$$x = -6$$

Practice Question

25) If $x + 15 = 4y$, and $y = 6$, what is the value of x?
   A. 5
   B. 6
   C. 7
   D. 8
   E. 9

26) Which of the following statements are valid steps in solving the equation 3x + 9 = 24? Select all correct answers.
   A. $12x = 24$
   B. $3x = 33$
   C. $3x = 15$
   D. $x = 2$
   E. $x = 5$

Word Problems

Mathematic expressions and equations can be used to model real-life situations. Often these situations are presented as **word problems** that can be translated from words into mathematical terms.

When working word problems, start by identifying the known and unknown values. Unknown values can be assigned a variable. Next, write an expression or equation that describes the mathematical relationship between those values. If necessary, the equation can then be solved.

Table 2.5 gives some common phrases and shows how they are translated into mathematical terms.

Table 2.5. Translating Word Problems		
Words	**Math Translation**	**Example**
equals, is, will be, yields	$=$	x is the same as y $x = y$
add, increase, added to, sum, combined, more than	$+$	2 more than x $x + 2$
minus, decreased, less than, subtracted, took away, difference between	$-$	3 less than x $x - 3$
multiplied by, times, product of	$\times$	the product of x and y $x \times y$
divided by, per, out of	$\div$	x divided by y $x \div y$

Practice Question

27) Joe's Rental Cars charges $35 plus 25 cents per mile to rent a car for one day. If Dan paid $90 to rent a car, how many miles did he drive?

28) Which problems below could be solved with the equation $12x + 15 = 195$? Select all correct answers.
  A. Marissa has $15. She wants to buy a stereo that costs $195. How much will Marissa need to save each month to be able to buy the stereo in a year?
  B. Jason has $15 and plans to save $15 per week. How long will it take him to have $195?
  C. Dana has $15 and plans to save $12 per week. How long will it take her to have $195?
  D. Casey has $15 and plans to save $195 per month. How much money will she have in a year?
  E. Nate spends $12, and now he has $195. How much money did he have to begin with?

Numerical and Graphic Relationships

Inequalities

An **inequality** shows the relationship between two expressions, much like an equation. However, the equal sign is replaced with an inequality symbol that expresses the following relationships:

< less than

> greater than

≤ less than or equal to

≥ greater than or equal to

Inequalities are read from left to right. For example, the inequality x < 8 would be read as "x is less than 8," meaning x has a value smaller than 8.

Linear inequalities can be solved in the same way as linear equations, with one exception. When multiplying or dividing both sides of an inequality by a negative number, the direction of the inequality sign must reverse—"greater than" becomes "less than" and "less than" becomes "greater than."

HELPFUL HINT

Equations have a finite number of solutions (e.g., $x = 3$).

Inequalities can have an infinite number of solutions, (e.g., $x < 4$).

Practice Question

29) Solve the following inequality for z: $3z + 10 < -z$.
  A. $z \geq 2.5$
  B. $z \leq 2.5$
  C. $z > -2.5$
  D. $z < -2.5$
  E. $z = 2.5$

Ordering Numbers

Some questions on the Math exam may require that numbers be compared or placed in ascending order. Below are some methods that can help make ordering numbers easier.

- For sets with fractions, give all the fractions a common denominator.

- For sets with fractions and decimals, convert all fractions to decimals. (Use the on-screen calculator if needed.)

- Place the numbers on a number line to visualize their relationship.

Practice Question

30) Which of the following numbers would create a list of numbers ordered from least to greatest if inserted in the blank space?

$\frac{1}{2}$, _____, 0.825

- A. 1.5
- B. 0
- C. $\frac{1}{3}$
- D. −0.75
- E. $\frac{4}{5}$

Types of Graphs

Bar graphs present the numbers of an item that exist in different categories. The categories are shown on one axis, and the number of items is shown on the other axis. Bar graphs are usually used to compare amounts easily.

Histograms similarly use bars to compare data, but the independent variable is a continuous variable that has been "binned" or divided into categories. For example, the time of day can be broken down into 8:00 a.m. to 12:00 p.m., 12:00 p.m. to 4:00 p.m., and so on. Usually (but not always), a gap is included between the bars of a bar graph but not a histogram.

Figure 2.15. Bar Graph versus Histogram

Scatter plots show the relationship between two sets of data by plotting the data as ordered pairs (x, y). One variable is plotted along the horizontal axis, and the second variable is plotted along the vertical axis.

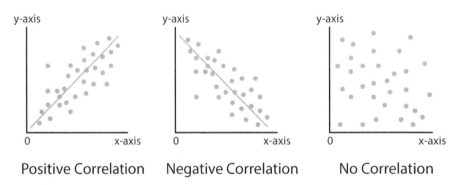

Figure 2.16. Scatter Plots and Correlation

HELPFUL HINT

In a line graph, each x-value corresponds to exactly one y-value. A scatter plot may have multiple y-values for one x-value.

The data in a scatter plot may show a **linear relationship** between the datasets. There is a **positive correlation** (expressed as a positive slope) if increasing one variable corresponds to an increase in the other variable. A **negative correlation** (expressed as a negative slope) occurs when an increase in one variable corresponds to a decrease in the other. If the scatter plot shows no discernible pattern, then there is no correlation (a zero, mixed, or indiscernible slope).

Correlation is a mathematical term that describes two variables that are statistically related (meaning one variable can be used to predict the other). **Causation** means that one variable directly influences another through a known mechanism. Correlation is not the same as causation: knowing two variables are statistically related does not mean one is directly influencing the other.

Line graphs are used to display a relationship between two continuous variables, such as change over time. Line graphs are constructed by graphing each point and connecting each point to the next consecutive point by a line.

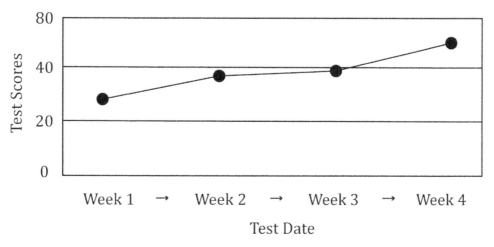

Figure 2.17. Line Graph

Pie charts show parts of a whole and are often used with percentages. Together, all the slices of the pie add up to the total number of items, or 100%.

Education Level of Applicants

Figure 2.18. Pie Chart

Stem-and-leaf plots are ways of organizing large amounts of data by grouping it into rows. All data points are broken into two parts: a stem and a leaf. For instance, the number 512 might be broken into a stem of 5 and a leaf of 12. All data in the 500 range would appear in the same row (this group of data is a class). The advantage of this display is that it shows general density and shape of the data in a compact display, yet all original data points are preserved and available. It is also easy to find medians and quartiles from this display.

Stem	Leaf
8	1 1 1 2 3 4 4 4 5 6 6 6 7 7 8 8 9
9	1 2 2

Figure 2.19. Stem and Leaf Plot

Practice Question

31) The graph below shows the average high temperature in Houston, Texas, for each month.

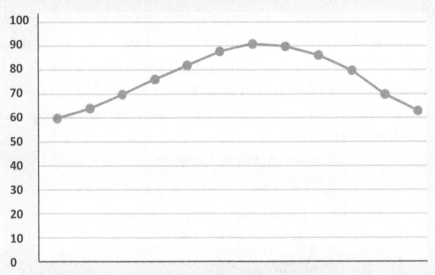

Which of the following is closest to the range for this data set?

A. 5
B. 15
C. 30
D. 60
E. 90

32) The stem-and-leaf plot below shows students' scores on a recent math test.

9	9, 8, 8, 5, 2, 1
8	8, 8, 8, 4, 2
7	9, 8, 6, 2
6	7, 7, 3
5	5

$$9|9 = 99$$

What was the median student score on the test?

A. 65
B. 84
C. 82
D. 88
E. 91

Answer Key

1) E: Most adults are between 1 and 2 meters tall. A kilometer and a mile are too large for measuring an adult's height. Pounds measure mass, and liters measure volume.

2) B: Use dimensional analysis.

$$\frac{10,000\ gal}{} \times \frac{1\ min}{x\ gal} = \frac{10,000}{x}\ minutes$$

3) D: This student drew a larger angle.

4) B: The formula for the area of a triangle is $\frac{1}{2}bh$, where b is the base and h is the height. In this triangle, y is the base and x is the height, so the triangle's area is $\frac{1}{2}xy$ or $\frac{xy}{2}$.

5) D: Find the area of the square without the cutouts; each side would be 12 mm long.

$$12mm \times 12mm = 144\ mm^2$$

Next, find the area of the cutouts.

$$2mm \times 2mm = 4mm^2$$
$$4 \times 4mm^2 = 16mm^2$$

Finally, subtract the total area of the four cutouts from the total area of the square without the cutouts.

$$144 - 16 = \mathbf{128\ mm^2}$$

6) 2 meters.

Use the formula for the volume of a rectangle solid to solve for the height (h).

$$V = wlh$$
$$30m^3 = (3m)(5m)(h)$$
$$\mathbf{h = 2\ meters}$$

7) E: Even though the problem does not give the four individual scores, it can be assumed that each test score was 81 (because four scores of 81 would average to 81). To find the score, x, that she needs:

$$\frac{4(81) + x}{5} = 83$$
$$324 + x = 415$$
$$x = 91$$

The student must score a 91 on the last test to have a mean score of 83.

8) 346. Range is the smallest value subtracted from the largest value.

$$418 - 72 = \mathbf{346}$$

2. Mathematics

9) B: Use the formula for probability.

$$P(an\ event) = \frac{number\ of\ favorable\ outcomes}{total\ number\ of\ possible\ outcomes}$$

$$= \frac{number\ of\ private\ school\ teachers}{total\ number\ of\ teachers}$$

$$= \frac{500{,}000}{3{,}200{,}000 + 500{,}000} = 0.14$$

$$= \mathbf{14\%}$$

10) B: The 8 is in the thousands place. Because the value to the right of the 8 is less than 5, the 8 remains the same and all values to its right become zero. The result is **498,000.**

11) C: Round each value and add.

$$129{,}113 \approx 129{,}000$$

$$34{,}602 \approx 35{,}000$$

$$129{,}000 + 35{,}000 = \mathbf{164{,}000}$$

12) A: Integers include both positive and negative numbers, while whole numbers are always positive (except zero). The number –5 is an integer but not a whole number because it is negative.

13) B: Because the temperature went down, add a negative number (or subtract).

$$-3 + -5 = \mathbf{-8°F}$$

14) C: Multiply the number of boxes by the number of pencils in each box to find the total number of pencils.

$$24 \times 110 = \mathbf{2640\ pencils}$$

15) C: First, simplify the expression in parentheses.

$$7 + 24 \div 8 \times (4 - 6)^2 = 7 + 24 \div 8 \times (-2)^2$$

Next, simplify the exponential expression.

$$7 + 24 \div 8 \times (-2)^2 = 7 + 24 \div 8 \times 4$$

Then, multiply and divide, working from left to right.

$$7 + 24 \div 8 \times 4 = 7 + 3 \times 4$$

$$7 + 3 \times 4 = 7 + 12$$

Finally, add: $7 + 12 = \mathbf{19}$

16) C: Find the factors of 12.

$$12 = 12 \times 1$$

$$12 = 6 \times 2$$

$$12 = 4 \times 3$$

Find the factors of 26.

$$26 = 26 \times 1$$
$$26 = 13 \times 2$$

The factors of 12 are **1, 2**, 3, 4, 6, and 12.

The factors of 26 are **1, 2**, 13, and 26.

The shaded region will contain the numbers 1 and 2.

17) C: 7 of 8 pizza slices are left after Carla takes 1, so $\frac{7}{8}$ of the pizza remains. **7** is the numerator of this fraction.

18) $\frac{3}{20}$. Find $\frac{1}{5}$ of $\frac{3}{4}$ by multiplying the fractions:

$$\frac{1}{5} \times \frac{3}{4} = \frac{3}{20}$$

19) D: $1.3208 \div 5.2 = 0.254$

The 5 is in the hundredths place.

20) 3:2. Find the number of women working at the company.

$$30 - 12 = 18 \; women$$

Write the ratio as the number of women over the number of men working at the company.

$$\frac{number\ of\ women}{number\ of\ men} = \frac{18}{12}$$

Reduce the ratio.

$$\frac{18 \div 6}{12 \div 6} = \frac{3}{2}$$

The ratio of women to men is $\frac{3}{2}$ or **3:2**.

21) B: Write a proportion using x for the missing value.

$$\frac{60\ kg}{90\ mg} = \frac{80\ kg}{x}$$

Cross-multiply and solve for x.

$$60(x) = 80(90)$$
$$60x = 7200$$
$$x = 120$$

The proper dosage is 120 mg.

22) 20. Set up a proportion and solve.

$$\frac{part}{whole} = \frac{\%}{100}$$

$$\frac{16}{x} = \frac{80}{100}$$

$$16(100) = 80(x)$$

$$\boldsymbol{x = 20}$$

23) A: Use the formula for percent change to find the sales price for each book.

$$amount\ of\ change = original\ amount \times percent\ change$$

$$amount\ of\ change = \$16 \times 0.08 = \$1.28$$

$$new\ price = \$16 + \$1.28 = \$17.28$$

To find the store owner's profit, subtract the amount he paid for the books from the amount he made selling them.

$$\$17.28(100) - \$16(100) = \boldsymbol{\$128}$$

24) D: Apply the distributive property to each term.

$$3x(x + 7) = 3x^2 + 21x$$

$$4x(2x - 6) = 8x^2 - 24x$$

Combine like terms.

$$(3x^2 + 21x) + (8x^2 - 24x) = 3x^2 + 8x^2 + 21x - 24x = \boldsymbol{11x^2 - 3x}$$

25) E: Substitute $y = 6$ into the equation.

$$x + 15 = 4y$$

$$x + 15 = 4(6)$$

$$x + 15 = 24$$

Subtract 15 from both sides to solve for x.

$$x + 15 - 15 = 24 - 15$$

$$\boldsymbol{x = 9}$$

26) C, E: Subtract 9 from both sides.

$$3x + 9 = 24$$

$$3x + 9 - 9 = 24 - 9$$

$$3x = 15$$

Divide both sides by 3.

$$\frac{3x}{3} = \frac{15}{3}$$

$$x = 5$$

27) 220. Represent the unknown quantity with a variable.

$$m = number\ of\ miles$$

Write an equation to represent the facts in the problem. The rental company will multiply the number of miles by 25 cents and add the $35 base charge.

$$0.25m + 35 = 90$$

Solve the equation.

$$0.25m = 55$$

$$m = 220$$

Dan drove 220 miles.

28) A, C: In choice A, x represents the amount of money Marissa will save each month. It is multiplied by 12 (because there are 12 months in a year) and added to the $15 she had to begin with, for a total of $195.

In choice C, x represents the number of weeks that Dana will save money. It is multiplied by $12 per week and added to the $15 she had to begin with, for a total of **$195.**

29) D: Isolate z by moving variable terms to one side and constants to the other.

$$3z + 10 < -z$$

$$3z < -z - 10$$

$$4z < -10$$

$$z < -2.5$$

30) E: Start by converting the fraction in the list to a decimal.

$$\frac{1}{2} = 0.5$$

The new list is now all decimals.

$$0.5, \_\_\_\_\_, 0.825$$

Now convert the other fractions to decimals.

$$\frac{1}{3} = 0.33 \ldots$$

$$\frac{4}{5} = 0.8$$

Find the decimal value that falls within 0.5 and 0.825.

$$0.5 < \mathbf{0.8} < 0.825$$

Choose the answer choice with the original fraction.

$$\frac{1}{2}, \frac{4}{5}, 0.825$$

31) C: The highest temperature is around 90°F, and the lowest temperature is around 60°F.

Subtract to find the range.

$$90 - 60 = \mathbf{30}$$

32) B: Count the number of scores: there are 19 total values in the set.

Count from the top or bottom to find the middle (10th) value.

9	9, 8, 8, 5, 2, 1
8	8, 8, 8, **4**, 2
7	9, 8, 6, 2
6	7, 7, 3
5	5

$9|9 = 99$

3. Writing

The CBEST Writing Test comprises two constructed-response questions— essays. You will be provided with two prompts. In one prompt, you must analyze a situation or statement, and on the other, you must describe a personal experience.

To do well on the Writing Test, take a clear side on the issue put forth in the prompt. Support your perspective with strong arguments and specific examples. An effective essay is clearly organized and structured, displays strong vocabulary, and features complex sentences.

Writing A Thesis Statement

A **thesis statement** articulates the main argument of the essay. No essay is complete without it: the structure and organization of the essay revolves around the thesis statement. The thesis statement is simply the writer's main idea or argument. It usually appears at the end of the introduction.

In a good thesis statement, the author states their idea or argument and why it is correct or true.

EXAMPLES
Take a position on the following topic in your essay. You can choose to write about either of the two viewpoints discussed in the prompt, or you may argue for a third point of view.

Many scientists argue that recent unusual weather patterns, such as powerful hurricanes and droughts, are due to climate change triggered by human activity.

They argue that automobiles, oil and gas production, and manufacturing generate carbon emissions that artificially heat the atmosphere, resulting in extreme weather patterns. Others disagree. Some researchers and media pundits argue that climate change is natural, and that extreme weather has always been a feature of Earth's atmosphere.

Possible thesis statements:

- Around the world more people than ever before are driving cars, and industrial production is at an all-time high: it is obvious that human activity is affecting the atmosphere and causing extreme weather events.

- I believe that temperatures and storms are more extreme than ever because of the environmental impact of human activity; not only do scientists have overwhelming evidence that climate change is unnatural, but I can also personally remember when there were fewer storms and variations in temperature.

- Society needs cars and manufacturing, but governments should restrict harmful emissions released into the atmosphere so we can slow down climate change and save lives.

Structuring the Essay

On the CBEST, a strong essay will have an introduction, a body, and a conclusion. While there are many ways to organize an essay, on this exam it is most important that the essay is clearly structured. There is no need to get too complicated: this simple structure will do.

Introductions

Some writers struggle with the introduction, but it is actually an opportunity to present your idea or argument. On the CBEST, the introduction can be one paragraph that ends with the thesis statement. In the rest of the paragraph, the writer provides some context for his or her argument. This context might include counterarguments, a preview of specific examples to be discussed later on, acknowledgment of the complexities of the issue, or even a reference to personal experience. The writer can reexamine some of these issues in the conclusion.

> **HELPFUL HINT**
>
> If you're not sure what to include in your introduction, start your essay with just the thesis statement. You can go back and complete the introduction once the rest of the essay is finished.

EXAMPLE

In the example below, the writer has written an introduction that includes context for her argument: background information, a counterargument, and personal experience. As a result, the reader has a better idea of how complex the issue is and why the writer feels the way she does. The thesis statement appears at the end of the paragraph; as a result of the introduction as a whole, the thesis statement has more impact.

A century ago, there were barely any cars on the road. Oil had just been discovered in a few parts of the world. Industrial production existed but had not yet exploded with the introduction of the assembly line. Refineries and factories were not yet churning out the chemical emissions they are today. Certainly, hurricanes and droughts occurred, but the populations and infrastructure affected were far smaller. Now, scientists have evidence that human activity—like pollution from industry and cars—is affecting the atmosphere and making weather more extreme. In 2017, millions of people were affected by hurricanes and wildfires. It is true that some researchers disagree that human activity has caused these and other extreme weather events. But why take the risk? If we can limit destruction now and in the future, we should. Extreme weather events are a danger to people all around the world. Society needs cars and manufacturing, but governments should restrict harmful emissions released into the atmosphere so we can slow down climate change and save lives.

The Body Paragraphs

Most writers find the body of the essay the easiest part to write. The body of the essay is simply several paragraphs, each beginning with a topic sentence. Each paragraph usually addresses an example that supports the argument made in the thesis statement or, in the case of an expository essay, explains the writer's reasoning. On the CBEST, you may use specific examples, personal anecdotes, present problems and solutions, or compare and contrast ideas. You do not need to refer to any outside literature or documentation.

To strengthen the body of the essay, writers will maintain consistency in paragraphs, always beginning with a topic sentence, which introduces the main idea of each paragraph. Each paragraph deals with its own main topic, but writers should use transition words and phrases to link paragraphs with each other. A good essay maintains readability and flow.

EXAMPLE

This example body paragraph is related to the introduction provided above. It provides reasoning and historical evidence for the author's argument that human activity is impacting the earth and causing climate change.

Human industrial activity has been growing exponentially, putting more pollution into the atmosphere than ever. Over the past forty years, large countries like China and India have become industrialized and manufacture many of the world's products. As their populations become more prosperous, demand for automobiles also rises, putting more cars on the road—and exhaust in the air. While industrial development has benefitted Asia and other areas, carbon emissions that cause climate change have multiplied. Meanwhile, previously industrialized countries in Europe and North America continue to produce carbon emissions. In the nineteenth century, only a few countries had industrial sectors; today, global industry strains the environment like never before. The past 150 years have seen unprecedented industrial growth. Even if the climate changes naturally over time, it cannot be denied that recent human activity has suddenly generated enormous amounts of carbon emissions that have impacted the atmosphere. Scientists say that the earth is warming as a result.

Conclusions

The conclusion does not need to be long. Its purpose is to wrap up the essay, reminding the reader why the topic and the writer's argument is important. It is an opportunity for the writer to reexamine the thesis statement and ideas in the introduction. It is a time to reinforce the argument, not just to repeat the introduction.

EXAMPLE

This example is taken from the same essay as the introduction and body paragraph above. It reinforces the writer's argument without simply repeating what she said in the introduction. The writer does address the topics she spoke about in the introduction (climate change and protecting people from extreme weather) but she does not simply rewrite the thesis: she calls for action.

No doubt, scientists, pundits, and politicians will continue to argue over the reasons for extreme weather. Meanwhile, Mother Nature will continue to wreak havoc on vulnerable areas regardless of what we think. Because we have proof that climate change is related to extreme weather and we know that extreme weather threatens people's lives, the time to act is now. We can take steps to mitigate pollution without lowering quality of life. Doing anything else is irresponsible—and for some, deadly.

Providing Supporting Evidence

As discussed above, a good essay should have specific evidence or examples that support the thesis statement. On the CBEST, a specific example should be something related to the idea of the paragraph and the essay, not a new idea. A specific example can be from your general knowledge; you do not need to know about specific academic issues to do well on the essay. Remember, you are being tested on your reasoning and argumentative skills.

The following are some examples of general statements and specific statements that provide more detailed support:

- **General:** Human industrial activity has been growing exponentially, putting more pollution into the atmosphere than ever.

- **Specific:** Over the past forty years, large countries like China and India have become industrialized and manufacture many of the world's products. As their populations become more prosperous, demand for automobiles also rises, putting more cars on the road—and exhaust in the air.

- **Specific:** Meanwhile, previously industrialized countries in Europe and North America continue to produce carbon emissions. In the nineteenth century, only a few countries had industrial sectors; today, global industry strains the environment like never before.

- **General:** More people than ever are affected by extreme weather.

- **Specific:** In 2017, several hurricanes affected the United States and the Caribbean. In Texas, Hurricane Harvey led to historic flooding in Houston and the Texas Coast. Millions of people were affected; thousands lost their homes, jobs, and livelihoods.

- **Specific:** Hurricane Irma damaged the US Virgin Islands and neighboring Caribbean nations. Soon after, Hurricane Maria catastrophically devastated Puerto Rico. Months later, Puerto Ricans were still without power and basic necessities. It is still not clear how many have died due to the storm and related damage.

EXAMPLE

In the example below, the paragraph is structured with a topic sentence and specific supporting ideas. This paragraph supports the introduction in the example above.

More people than ever are affected by extreme weather. In 2017, several hurricanes affected the United States and the Caribbean. In Texas, Hurricane Harvey led to historic flooding in Houston and the Texas Coast. Millions of people were affected; thousands lost their homes, jobs, and livelihoods. Hurricane Irma damaged Florida, the US Virgin Islands and neighboring Caribbean nations. Soon after, Hurricane Maria catastrophically devastated Puerto Rico. Months later, Puerto Ricans were still without power and basic necessities. It is still not clear how many have died due to the storm and related damage. In California, severe droughts led to exceptionally large wildfires that threatened Los Angeles and destroyed neighboring communities. Meanwhile, those same areas—Southern California, the Texas Coast, and Florida—continue to grow, putting more people at risk when the next hurricane or fire strikes.

Writing Well

Using transitions, complex sentences, and certain words can turn a good essay into a great one. Transitions, syntax, word choice, and tone all help clarify and amplify a writer's argument or point and improve the flow of an essay.

Transitions

An essay consists of several paragraphs. **Transitions** are words and phrases that help connect the paragraphs and ideas of the text. Most commonly, transitions would appear at the beginning of a paragraph, but writers should also use them throughout a text to connect ideas. Common transitions are words like *also, next, still, although, in addition to*, and *in other words*. A transition shows a relationship between ideas, so writers should pay close attention to the transition words and phrases they choose. Transitions may show connections or contrasts between words and ideas.

Table 3.1. Common Transitions	
Transition Type	**Examples**
addition	additionally, also, as well, further, furthermore, in addition, moreover
cause/effect	as a result, because, consequently, due to, if/then, so, therefore, thus
concluding	briefly, finally, in conclusion, in summary, thus, to conclude
contrast	but, however, in contrast, nevertheless, on the contrary, on the other hand, yet
examples	for example, for instance, in other words
similarity	also, likewise, similarly
time	after, before, currently, later, recently, since, subsequently, then, while

Syntax

Syntax refers to how words and phrases are arranged in writing or speech. Writing varied sentences is essential to capturing and keeping a reader's interest. A good essay features different types of sentences: simple, complex, compound, and compound complex. Sentences need not always begin with the subject; they might start with a transition word or phrase, for instance. Variety is key.

Still, writers should keep in mind that the point of an essay is to get an idea across to the reader, so it is most important that writing be clear. They should not sacrifice clarity for the sake of flowery, overly wordy language or confusing syntax.

Word Choice and Tone

Like syntax, **word choice** makes an impression on readers. The CBEST does not test on specific vocabulary or require writers to use specific words on the essay. However, the essay is a good opportunity to use strong vocabulary pertaining to the prompt or issue under discussion. Writers should be careful, though, that they understand the words they are using. Writers should also avoid vague, imprecise, or generalizing language like *good, bad, a lot, a little, very, normal*, and so on.

Editing, Revising, and Proofreading

On the CBEST, the writer has a limited amount of time to complete the essay. If there is time for editing or proofreading, writers should hunt for grammar, spelling, or punctuation mistakes that could change the meaning of the text or make it difficult to understand. These include sentence fragments, run-on sentences, subject-verb disagreement, and pronoun-antecedent disagreement.

Practice Test #1

Reading

Read the passage or graphic, and then answer the questions that follow.

Use the following passage for questions 1–5.

In recent decades, jazz has been associated with New Orleans and festivals like Mardi Gras, but in the 1920s, jazz was a booming trend whose influence reached into many aspects of American culture. In fact, the years between World War I and the Great Depression were known as the Jazz Age, a term coined by F. Scott Fitzgerald in his famous novel *The Great Gatsby*. Sometimes also called the Roaring Twenties, this time period saw major urban centers experiencing new economic, cultural, and artistic vitality. In the United States, musicians flocked to cities like New York and Chicago, which became famous hubs for jazz musicians. Ella Fitzgerald, for example, moved from Virginia to New York City to begin her much-lauded singing career, and jazz pioneer Louis Armstrong got his big break in Chicago.

Jazz music was played by and for a more expressive and freed populace than the United States had previously seen. Women gained the right to vote and were openly seen drinking and dancing to jazz music. This period marked the emergence of the flapper, a woman determined to make a statement about her new role in society. Jazz music also provided the soundtrack for the explosion of African American art and culture now known as the Harlem Renaissance. In addition to Fitzgerald and Armstrong, numerous musicians, including Duke Ellington, Fats Waller, and Bessie Smith, promoted their distinctive and complex music as an integral part of the emerging African American culture.

1. What is the main idea of the passage?
    A.   People should associate jazz music with the 1920s, not modern New Orleans.
    B.   Jazz music played an important role in many cultural movements of the 1920s.
    C.   Many famous jazz musicians began their careers in New York City and Chicago.
    D.   African Americans were instrumental in launching jazz into mainstream culture.
    E.   The Jazz Age was a period of cultural and artistic exuberance, which had little economic or political significance.

2. The passage supports which of the following claims about jazz music?
    A.   Jazz music was important to minority groups struggling for social equality in the 1920s.
    B.   Duke Ellington, Fats Waller, and Bessie Smith were the most important jazz musicians of the Harlem Renaissance.
    C.   Women gained the right to vote with the help of jazz musicians.
    D.   Duke Ellington, Fats Waller, and Bessie Smith all supported women's right to vote.
    E.   The success of jazz music contributed to a spike in America's economic wealth.

3. The primary purpose of the passage is to
   A.   explain the role jazz musicians played in the Harlem Renaissance.
   B.   inform the reader about the many important musicians playing jazz in the 1920s.
   C.   discuss how jazz influenced important cultural movements in the 1920s.
   D.   provide a history of jazz music in the 20th century.
   E.   describe how jazz music and the Roaring Twenties are depicted in modern-day popular culture.

4. Which of the following is NOT a fact stated in the passage?
   A.   The years between World War I and the Great Depression were known as the Jazz Age.
   B.   Ella Fitzgerald and Louis Armstrong both moved to New York City to start their music careers.
   C.   Women danced to jazz music during the 1920s to make a statement about their role in society.
   D.   Jazz music was an integral part of the emerging African American culture of the 1920s.
   E.   In modern-day popular culture, jazz music is most often associated with New Orleans and Mardi Gras.

5. Which conclusion about jazz music is supported by the passage?
   A.   F. Scott Fitzgerald supported jazz musicians in New York and Chicago.
   B.   Jazz music is no longer as popular as it once was.
   C.   Both women and African Americans used jazz music as a way of expressing their newfound freedom.
   D.   Flappers and African American musicians worked together to produce jazz music.
   E.   Jazz music was a direct result of the economic wealth the country was experiencing at the time.

Use the following passage for question 6.

It has now been two decades since the introduction of thermonuclear fusion weapons into the military inventories of the great powers, and more than a decade since the United States, Great Britain, and the Soviet Union ceased to test nuclear weapons in the atmosphere. Today our understanding of the technology of thermonuclear weapons seems highly advanced, but our knowledge of the physical and biological consequences of nuclear war is continuously evolving.

6. The passage is primarily concerned with
   A.   the impact of thermonuclear weapons on the military.
   B.   the technology of thermonuclear weapons.
   C.   atmospheric testing of nuclear weapons.
   D.   the physical and biological consequences of nuclear war.
   E.   the nuclear ceasefire between the United States, Great Britain, and the Soviet Union.

Use the following passage for question 7.

In Greek mythology, two gods, Epimetheus and Prometheus, were given the work of creating living things. Epimetheus gave good powers to the different animals. To the lion he gave strength; to the bird, swiftness; to the fox, sagacity; and so on. Eventually, all of the good gifts had been bestowed, and there was nothing left for humans. As a result, Prometheus returned to heaven and brought down fire, which he gave to humans. With fire, human beings could protect themselves by making weapons. Over time, humans developed civilization.

7. As used in the passage, "bestowed" most nearly means
    A. purchased.
    B. forgotten.
    C. accepted.
    D. given.
    E. lost.

Use the following passage for questions 8–10.

It could be said that the great battle between the North and South we call the Civil War was a battle for individual identity. The states of the South had their own culture, one based on farming, independence, and the rights of both man and state to determine their own paths. Similarly, the North had forged its own identity as a center of centralized commerce and manufacturing. This clash of lifestyles was bound to create tension, and this tension was bound to lead to war. But people who try to sell you this narrative are wrong. The Civil War was not a battle of cultural identities—it was a battle about slavery. All other explanations for the war are either a direct consequence of the South's desire for wealth at the expense of her fellow man or a fanciful invention to cover up this sad portion of our nation's history. And it cannot be denied that this time in our past was very sad indeed.

8. As used in the passage, "fanciful" most nearly means
    A. complicated.
    B. imaginative.
    C. successful.
    D. unfortunate.
    E. opulent.

9. The primary purpose of the passage is to
    A. convince readers that slavery was the main cause of the Civil War.
    B. illustrate the cultural differences between the North and the South before the Civil War.
    C. persuade readers that the North deserved to win the Civil War.
    D. demonstrate that the history of the Civil War is too complicated to be understood clearly.
    E. describe the various causes of the American Civil War.

10. What is the main idea of the passage?
    A. The Civil War was the result of cultural differences between the North and South.
    B. The Civil War was caused by the South's reliance on slave labor.
    C. The North's use of commerce and manufacturing allowed it to win the war.
    D. The South's belief in the rights of man and state cost the war.
    E. America's reliance on slave labor in the centuries before the Civil War is a sad and shameful part of the country's history.

Use the following passage for question 11.

After looking at five houses, Robert and I have decided to buy the one on Forest Road. The first two homes we visited didn't have the space we need—the first had only one bathroom, and the second did not have a guest bedroom. The third house, on Pine Street, had enough space inside but didn't have a big enough yard for our three dogs. The fourth house we looked at, on Rice Avenue, was stunning but well above our price range. The last home, on Forest Road, wasn't in the neighborhood we wanted to live in. However, it had the right amount of space for the right price.

11. What is the author's conclusion about the house on Pine Street?
    A.   The house did not have enough bedrooms.
    B.   The house did not have a big enough yard.
    C.   The house was not in the right neighborhood.
    D.   The house was too expensive.
    E.   The house had the right amount of space for the right price.

Use the following passage for question 12.

For an adult to be unable to swim is criminal negligence: every man, woman, and child should learn. A person who cannot swim is a danger not only to himself but also to the people around him. Children as early as the age of four may acquire the art; no one is too young or too old.

12. Which of the following best captures the author's purpose?
    A.   to encourage the reader to learn to swim
    B.   to explain how people who cannot swim are a danger to others
    C.   to inform the reader that it is never too late to learn to swim
    D.   to argue that people who cannot swim should be punished
    E.   to describe an effective way to teach swimming to adults

Use the following passage and graphic *for questions 13 and 14.*

As you can see from the graph, my babysitting business has been really successful. The year started with a busy couple of months—several snows combined with a large number of requests for Valentine's Day services boosted our sales quite a bit. The spring months have admittedly been a bit slow, but we're hoping for a big summer once school gets out. Several clients have already put in requests for our services!

13. Based on the information in the graph, how much more did Sam's Babysitting Service bring in during February than during April?

Sam's Net Income by Month

A. $200
B. $900
C. $1,100
D. $1,300
E. $1,800

14. Which of the following best describes the tone of the passage?
A. professional
B. casual
C. concerned
D. neutral
E. disheartened

Use the following passage for questions 15–19.

Taking a person's temperature is one of the most basic and common health care tasks. Everyone from nurses to emergency medical technicians to concerned parents should be able to grab a thermometer to take a patient or loved one's temperature. But what's the best way to get an accurate reading? The answer depends on the situation.

The most common way people measure body temperature is orally. A simple digital or disposable thermometer is placed under the tongue for a few minutes, and the task is done. There are many situations, however, when measuring temperature orally isn't an option. For example, when a person can't breathe through the nose, they won't be able to keep their mouth closed long enough to get an accurate reading. In these situations, it's often preferable to place the thermometer in the rectum or armpit. Using the rectum also has the added benefit of providing a much more accurate reading than other locations can provide.

In addition, certain people, like agitated patients or fussy babies, won't be able to sit still long enough for an accurate reading. In these situations, it's best to use a thermometer that works much more quickly, such as one that measures temperature in the ear or at the temporal artery. No matter which method is chosen, however, it's important to check the average temperature for each region, as it can vary by several degrees.

15. Which statement is NOT a fact from the passage?
   A. Taking a temperature in the ear or at the temporal artery is more accurate than taking it orally.
   B. If an individual cannot breathe through the nose, taking their temperature orally will likely give an inaccurate reading.
   C. The standard human body temperature varies depending on whether it's measured in the mouth, rectum, armpit, ear, or temporal artery.
   D. The most common way to measure temperature is by placing a thermometer in the mouth.
   E. Some patients are unable to sit still long enough for an accurate reading using an oral thermometer.

16. The primary purpose of the passage is to
   A. advocate for the use of thermometers that measure temperature in the ear or at the temporal artery.
   B. explain the methods available to measure a person's temperature and the situation where each method is appropriate.
   C. warn readers that the average temperature of the human body varies by region.
   D. discuss how nurses use different types of thermometers depending on the type of patient they are examining.
   E. inform readers of the proper procedure for taking a baby's temperature.

17. Which of the following is the best summary of this passage?
   A. It's important that everyone know the best way to take a person's temperature in any given situation.
   B. The most common method of taking a person's temperature—orally—isn't appropriate in some situations.
   C. The most accurate way to take a temperature is placing a digital thermometer in the rectum.
   D. There are many different ways to take a person's temperature, and which is appropriate will depend on the situation.
   E. Nurses and parents must take special steps when taking the temperatures of fussy babies.

18. As used in the passage, "agitated" most nearly means
   A. obviously upset.
   B. quickly moving.
   C. violently ill.
   D. slightly dirty.
   E. physically comfortable.

19. According to the passage, why is it sometimes preferable to take a person's temperature rectally?
    A.   Rectal readings are more accurate than oral readings.
    B.   Many people cannot sit still long enough to have their temperatures taken orally.
    C.   Temperature readings can vary widely between regions of the body.
    D.   Many people do not have access to quick-acting thermometers.
    E.   People who are ill may not be able to sit still long enough to have their temperatures taken through their ears or temporal arteries.

Use the following passage for question 20.

When the Spanish-American War broke out in 1898, the US Army was small and understaffed. President William McKinley called for 1,250 volunteers, primarily from the Southwest, to serve in the First US Volunteer Cavalry. Eager to fight, the ranks were quickly filled by a diverse group of cowboys, gold prospectors, hunters, gamblers, Native Americans, veterans, police officers, and college students looking for an adventure. The officer corps was composed of veterans of the Civil War and the Indian Wars. With more volunteers than it could accept, the army set high standards: all the recruits had to be skilled on horseback and with guns. Consequently, they became known as the Rough Riders.

20. According to the passage, all the recruits were required to
    A.   have previously fought in a war.
    B.   be American citizens.
    C.   live in the Southwest.
    D.   ride a horse well.
    E.   have a college degree.

Use the following passage for questions 21–26.

Popcorn is often associated with fun and festivities, both in and out of the home. It's eaten in theaters, usually after being salted and smothered in butter, and in homes, fresh from the microwave. But popcorn isn't just for fun—it's also a multimillion-dollar-a-year industry with a long and fascinating history.

While popcorn might seem like a modern invention, its history actually dates back thousands of years, making it one of the oldest snack foods enjoyed around the world. Popcorn is believed by food historians to be one of the earliest uses of cultivated corn. In 1948, Herbert Dick and Earle Smith discovered old popcorn dating back 4,000 years in the New Mexico Bat Cave. For the Aztec Indians who called the caves home, popcorn (or momochitl) played an important role in society, both as a food staple and in ceremonies. The Aztecs cooked popcorn by heating sand in a fire; when it was heated, kernels were added and would pop when exposed to the heat of the sand.

The American love affair with popcorn began in 1912, when popcorn was first sold in theaters. The popcorn industry flourished during the Great Depression when it was advertised as a wholesome and economical food. Selling for five to ten cents a bag, it was a luxury that the downtrodden could afford. With the introduction of mobile popcorn machines at the World's Columbian Exposition, popcorn moved from the theater into fairs and parks. Popcorn continued to rule the snack food kingdom until the rise in popularity of home televisions during the 1950s.

The popcorn industry reacted to the decline in sales quickly by introducing pre-popped and unpopped popcorn for home consumption. However, it wasn't until microwave popcorn became commercially available in 1981 that at-home popcorn consumption began to grow exponentially. With the wide availability of microwaves in the United States, popcorn also began popping up in offices and hotel rooms. However, the home still remains the most popular popcorn eating spot: today, 70 percent of the 16 billion quarts of popcorn consumed annually in the United States are eaten at home.

21. The passage supports which of the following claims about popcorn?
   A. People ate less popcorn in the 1950s than in previous decades because they went to the movies less.
   B. Without mobile popcorn machines, people would not have been able to eat popcorn during the Great Depression.
   C. People enjoyed popcorn during the Great Depression because it was a luxury food.
   D. During the 1800s, people began abandoning theaters to go to fairs and festivals.
   E. Today, popcorn is a popular snack food because of its wholesomeness and affordability.

22. As used in the passage, "staple" most nearly means
   A. something produced only for special occasions.
   B. something produced regularly in large quantities.
   C. something produced by cooking.
   D. something fastened together securely.
   E. something of high nutritional value.

23. The primary purpose of the passage is to
   A. explain how microwaves affected the popcorn industry.
   B. show that popcorn is older than many people realize.
   C. illustrate the history of popcorn from ancient cultures to modern times.
   D. demonstrate the importance of popcorn in various cultures.
   E. highlight the large increase in profits that the popcorn industry has seen in recent decades.

24. Which factor does the author of the passage credit for the growth of the popcorn industry in the United States?
   A. the use of popcorn in ancient Aztec ceremonies
   B. the growth of the home television industry
   C. the marketing of popcorn during the Great Depression
   D. the nutritional value of popcorn
   E. the introduction of pre-popped and unpopped popcorn to the market

25. What is the best summary of this passage?
   A. Popcorn is a popular snack food that dates back thousands of years. Its popularity in the United States has been tied to the growth of theaters and the availability of microwaves.
   B. Popcorn has been a popular snack food for thousands of years. Archaeologists have found evidence that many ancient cultures used popcorn as a food staple and in ceremonies.
   C. Popcorn was first introduced to America in 1912, and its popularity has grown exponentially since then. Today, over 16 billion quarts of popcorn are consumed in the United States annually.
   D. Popcorn is a versatile snack food that can be eaten with butter or other toppings. It can also be cooked in a number of different ways, including in microwaves.
   E. Popcorn is a versatile snack food that can be enjoyed in any number of locations such as theaters, festivals, at home, and even at work.

26. Which of the following is NOT a fact stated in the passage?
    A. Archaeologists have found popcorn dating back 4,000 years.
    B. Popcorn was first sold in theaters in 1912.
    C. Consumption of popcorn dropped in 1981 with the growing popularity of home televisions.
    D. Seventy percent of the popcorn consumed in the United States is eaten in homes.
    E. The popcorn industry flourished during the Great Depression.

Use the following passage for question 27.

The *Scream of Nature* by Edvard Munch is one of the world's best known and most desirable artworks. While most people think of it as a single painting, the iconic creation actually has four different versions: two paintings and two pastels. In 2012, one of the pastels earned the fourth highest price paid for a painting at auction when it was sold for almost $120 million. The three others are not for sale; the Munch Museum in Oslo holds a painted version and a pastel version, while the National Gallery in Oslo holds the other painting. However, the desire to acquire them has been just as strong: in 1994 the National Gallery's version was stolen, and in 2004 the painting at the Munch Museum was stolen at gunpoint in the middle of the day. Both paintings were eventually recovered.

27. The primary purpose of the passage is to
    A. describe the image depicted in The Scream in Nature.
    B. explain the origin of the painting The Scream in Nature.
    C. clarify the number of versions of The Scream in Nature that exist.
    D. prove the high value of The Scream in Nature.
    E. outline the different ownerships of The Scream in Nature.

Use the following passage for questions 28–30.

In its most basic form, geography is the study of space; more specifically, it studies the physical space of the earth and the ways in which it interacts with, shapes, and is shaped by its inhabitants. Geographers look at the world from a spatial perspective. This means that at the center of all geographic study is the question, where? For geographers, the where of any interaction, event, or development is a crucial element to understanding it.

This question of where can be asked in a variety of fields of study, so there are many subdisciplines of geography. These can be organized into four main categories: (1) regional studies, which examine the characteristics of a particular place; (2) topical studies, which look at a single physical or human feature that impacts the whole world; (3) physical studies, which focus on the physical features of Earth; and (4) human studies, which examine the relationship between human activity and the environment.

28. A researcher studying the relationship between farming and river systems would be engaged in which of the following geographical subdisciplines?
    A. regional studies
    B. topical studies
    C. physical studies
    D. human studies
    E. physical and human studies

29. Which of the following best describes the mode of the passage?
    A. expository
    B. narrative
    C. persuasive
    D. descriptive
    E. rhetorical

30. Which of the following is a concise summary of the passage?
    A. The most important question in geography is where an event or development took place.
    B. Geography, which is the study of the physical space on Earth, can be broken down into four subdisciplines.
    C. Regional studies is the study of a single region or area.
    D. Geography can be broken down into four subdisciplines: regional studies, topical studies, physical studies, and human studies.
    E. The relationship between humans and their physical space is an important one.

Use the following passage for question 31.

After World War I, powerful political and social forces pushed for a return to normalcy in the United States. The result was disengagement from the larger world and increased focus on American economic growth and personal enjoyment. Caught in the middle of this was a cache of American writers, raised on the values of the prewar world and frustrated with what they viewed as the superficiality and materialism of postwar American culture. Many of them, like Ernest Hemingway and F. Scott Fitzgerald, fled to Paris, where they became known as the "lost generation," creating a trove of literary works criticizing their home culture and delving into their own feelings of alienation.

31. In the third sentence, the word "cache" most nearly means
    A. a group of the same type.
    B. a majority segment.
    C. an organization.
    D. a dispersed number.
    E. a new school.

Use the following passages *for questions 32–40.*

Passage 1

In the field of veterinary medicine, the inquiry into whether animals experience pain the same way humans do is especially important in the context of pain management. Although many advancements have been made in research sciences and pain management is widely accepted as a necessary job of practitioners, a number of myths about animal pain still plague the field of veterinary medicine and prevent practitioners from making pain management a priority. According to veterinarian and writer Debbie Grant, three myths are especially detrimental to the cause.

The first is the myth that animals do not feel pain at all or that they feel it less intensely than humans; in fact, according to Grant, the biological mechanisms by which we experience pain are the very same mechanisms by which animals experience pain. Even the emotional reaction to a painful experience, like being afraid to return to the dentist after an unpleasant visit, is mirrored in animals.

The second myth that prevents the advancement of pain management practices is the myth that pain is a necessary part of an animal's recovery. While some veterinarians believe that pain may prevent a healing dog, for example, from playing too vigorously, Grant says this is simply not the case. In fact, restlessness and discomfort may even lead to unusually high levels of agitation and may consequently slow the recovery process even further.

Finally, contrary to the third myth, animals do not necessarily tolerate pain any better than humans do, though they may handle their pain differently. Grant emphasizes that veterinarians must be aware that a lack of obvious signs does not necessarily suggest that pain is not present: in fact, many animals are likely to conceal their pain out of an instinct to hide weaknesses that may make them easy targets for predators.

Passage 2

Unlike doctors, who typically have the benefit of discussing their patients' concerns, veterinarians cannot ask their patients whether and where they are experiencing discomfort. Additionally, veterinarians must be aware of the survival instinct of many animals to mask pain in response to the foreign environment of a veterinary office. For these reasons, diagnostic tools and strategies are instrumental in the effective practice of veterinary medicine.

Veterinarians have a unique challenge when it comes to diagnosing their patients. In 2014, researchers of veterinary medicine at the University of Perugia in Italy completed a review of the diagnostic tools and strategies available to today's practitioners and found a number of them to be effective. Presumptive diagnosis, the first of these strategies, involves making a prediction about the animal's pain based on the observable damage to the body or body part. In addition to presumptive diagnosis, veterinarians can use close observation to assess changes in the animal's behavior.

The most common tool for performing diagnosis is the clinical exam, which can include both a physical exam and laboratory testing. As part of this process, a veterinarian might make use of an objective pain scale, by which he or she could assess the animal's condition according to a number of criteria. This tool is especially useful throughout the course of treatment, as it provides the practitioner with a quantitative measure for evaluating the effectiveness of various treatment options.

32. As it is used in Passage 1, the term "detrimental" most nearly mean
    A. mischievous.
    B. damaging.
    C. disturbing.
    D. advantageous.
    E. confusing.

33. The author of Passage 1 most likely includes the example of the unpleasant dentist visit in order to
    A. provide a relatable example of how pain can influence a person's emotions.
    B. challenge the reader to overcome his or her natural, emotional response to painful experiences.
    C. question a popular perception about the experience of going to the dentist.
    D. highlight a similarity in the way humans and animals respond to pain.
    E. remind the reader of how scary the dentist is for children.

34. As it is used in Passage 2, the term "foreign" most nearly means
   A. unfamiliar.
   B. inaccessible.
   C. distant.
   D. exotic.
   E. dangerous.

35. The author of Passage 1 indicates that despite advancements in veterinary sciences, many veterinarians
   A. do not see the value in pain management practices for their patients.
   B. still employ outdated methods of pain management.
   C. still believe that pain management is a responsibility of the pet owner.
   D. still have misguided beliefs and practices related to pain management in animals.
   E. do not have the technology to provide effective pain management options.

36. The author of Passage 2 indicates that veterinarians can improve their pain management practices by
   A. attempting to communicate with their patients about the pain they are experiencing.
   B. employing the best diagnostic practices in their field.
   C. encouraging pet owners to keep careful watch over their animals.
   D. inventing novel ways to assess and treat pain in animals.
   E. focusing on the causes of the pain rather than pain itself.

37. The author of Passage 2 indicates that objective pain measures are useful because
   A. they allow the veterinarian to compare an animal's pain level to the pain levels of other animals.
   B. they challenge the veterinarian to devise a treatment plan as quickly as possible.
   C. they discount the assumption that pain cannot be measured on an objective scale.
   D. they provide the veterinarian with a quantitative method for tracking pain levels over the course of an animal's treatment.
   E. they offer a new perspective on the management of pain in small animals.

38. The author of Passage 1 would most likely respond to the discussion of presumptive diagnosis in Passage 2 by
   A. asserting that substantial physical damage to an animal's form does not necessarily suggest the presence of pain.
   B. asserting that presumptive diagnosis is more effective for diagnosing humans and should not be used for diagnosing animals.
   C. asserting that similarities in methods of pain diagnosis for humans and animals are effective because of the biological similarities between them.
   D. asserting that veterinarians should not make use of presumptive diagnosis in evaluating and treating patients.
   E. asserting that the pain diagnosis is much more difficult in humans than in animals.

39. Which of the following best describes the relationship between the two passages?
    A. The first passage makes the claim that pain management should be a priority for veterinarians, while the second passage rejects this claim.
    B. The first passage emphasizes the veterinarian's responsibility to prioritize pain management in animals, while the second passage explores the tools by which veterinarians can execute this responsibility.
    C. The first passage seeks to dispel myths about pain management in animals, while the second passage denies that they are myths.
    D. The first passage sheds light on the shortcomings of veterinary sciences as they currently exist, while the second passage provides insight into how these shortcomings might be overcome.
    E. The first passage describes early approaches to pain management in animals, while the second passage highlights more modern approaches.

40. Both authors indicate that veterinarians
    A. must be aware that a lack of obvious symptoms does not necessarily suggest an absence of pain.
    B. should make pain management for their patients a priority.
    C. ought to be familiar with the misguided assumptions that exist in their field.
    D. need to conduct a thorough examination before releasing an animal back to its owner.
    E. should prioritize oral health care in order to prevent the need for painful procedures.

Use the following graph for question 41.

END-OF-YEAR GRADE REPORT

41. Which conclusion can be drawn from the graph?
    A. More than twice as many students earned an A in science than earned an F in science.
    B. The majority of the students earned a C in math.
    C. The number of students who earned a B in reading is equal to the number of students who earned a B in math.
    D. Next year's students will not need intensive science instruction.
    E. More students earned a C in science than earned a D in science.

Use the following passage for question 42.

One of the most dramatic acts of nonviolent resistance in India's movement for independence from Britain came in 1930, when independence leader Mahatma Gandhi organized a 240-mile march to the Arabian Sea. The goal of the march was to make salt from seawater, in defiance of British law. The British prohibited Indians from collecting or selling salt—a vital part of the Indian diet—requiring them instead to buy it from British merchants and pay a heavy salt tax. The crowd of marchers grew along the way to tens of thousands of people. In Dandi, Gandhi picked up a small chunk of salt and broke British law. Thousands in Dandi followed his lead as did millions of fellow protestors in coastal towns throughout India. In an attempt to quell the civil disobedience, authorities arrested more than 60,000 people across the country, including Gandhi himself.

42. With which of the following claims about civil disobedience would the author most likely agree?
    A. Civil disobedience is a disorganized form of protest easily quashed by government.
    B. Civil disobedience requires extreme violations of existing law to be effective.
    C. Civil disobedience is an effective strategy for effecting political change.
    D. Civil disobedience is only effective in countries that already have democracy.
    E. Civil disobedience can only work on a small scale to effect local change.

Use the following passage for questions 43–45.

Vexillology, the study of flags, became its own field of study in the mid-twentieth century. Who studies flags? Historians, sociologists, designers, and those simply interested in these ubiquitous signals. Flags are everywhere: homeowners fly them from their houses, balconies, or poles on lawns. Government buildings display them prominently.

Many people first think of flags that represent nationality. But there are other types of flags, too. For instance, coastal authorities may display flags at the beach indicating conditions for swimming and boating. Similarly, various flags are used by boaters to communicate on the high seas. Sports fans may wave the flags of their favorite teams at the game or display these flags at their homes. Still, most flags are indeed associated with a country, and there are over two hundred countries and territories on Earth today.

With so many different flags, it makes sense that the International Federation of Vexillogical Associations (which uses the acronym FIAV, reflecting its French name) meets to organize flag study and safeguard flag history. According to the FIAV, vexillology became an organized field in response to the decolonization and revolutionary movements of the 1960s, when many countries became independent for the first time. There was a need to keep track of new flags, so volunteers stepped up and the organization grew. Today, FIAV comprises several national associations of vexillology and meets regularly to discuss topics of interest.

43. As used in the passage, "prominently" most nearly means
    A. occasionally.
    B. visibly.
    C. rarely.
    D. outside.
    E. fashionably.

44. What is the main idea of this passage?
    A. It is important to study flags because countries use them.
    B. Vexillology and flags are controlled by one major group: the FIAV.
    C. The FIAV helps keep track of the many types of flags in the world today.
    D. Flags are only used to identify countries.
    E. The United Nations decides which countries may use which flags.

45. The reader can infer that "there was a need to keep track of new flags" following the decolonization period of the 1960s because
    A. many countries became independent around the same time and adopted national flags, causing a need for organization to avoid duplicates and other problems.
    B. due to the instability during the era of decolonization and revolutions, countries were at war over many issues, including flag design.
    C. an international organization was needed to grant flags to the many new countries that had gained independence.
    D. a number of new flags were issued to enhance communication on the high seas, now that more independent countries existed.
    E. more people became interested in vexillology during this time.

Use the following passage for question 46.

When a fire destroyed San Francisco's American Indian Center in October of 1969, American Indian groups set their sights on the recently closed island prison of Alcatraz as a site of a new Indian cultural center and school. Ignored by the government, an activist group known as Indians of All Tribes sailed to Alcatraz in the early morning hours with eighty-nine men, women, and children. They landed on Alcatraz, claiming it for all the tribes of North America. Their demands were ignored, so the group continued to occupy the island for the next nineteen months, its numbers swelling up to six hundred as others joined. By January of 1970, many of the original protestors had left, and on June 11, 1971, federal marshals forcibly removed the last residents.

46. The main idea of this passage is that
    A. the government refused to listen to the demands of American Indians.
    B. American Indians occupied Alcatraz in protest of government policy.
    C. few people joined the occupation of Alcatraz, weakening its effectiveness.
    D. the government took violent action against protestors at Alcatraz.
    E. American Indians wanted Alcatraz to be a new cultural center.

Use the following passage for question 47.

Increasingly, companies are turning to subcontracting services rather than hiring full-time employees. This provides companies with many advantages like greater flexibility, reduced legal responsibility to employees, and lower possibility of unionization within the company. However, it has also led to increasing confusion and uncertainty over the legal definition of employment. Recently, the courts have grappled with questions about the hiring company's responsibility in maintaining fair labor practices. Companies argue that they delegate that authority to the subcontractors, while unions and other worker advocate groups argue that companies still have a legal obligation to the workers who contribute to their business.

47. The primary purpose of the passage is to
    A. critique the labor practices of modern companies.
    B. explain why companies prefer subcontracting work.
    C. highlight a debate within the business and labor community.
    D. describe a recent court decision related to labor practices.
    E. provide evidence for the benefits of subcontracting to workers.

Use the following excerpt for questions 48 and 49.

Table of Contents

1. Renaissance Art ....15 – 104

   A) Italian Painters ....17 – 57

   B) German Painters ....59 – 72

   C) French Painters...73 – 104

2. Renaissance Architecture ....105 – 203

   A) Renaissance: 1400 – 1500...107 – 152

   B) High Renaissance: 1500 – 1525.............................153 – 177

   C) Mannerism: 1520 – 1600 ....179 – 203

48. A student wants to find information on the Italian painter Sandro Botticelli. On which of the following pages will the student most likely find this information?
    A. 55
    B. 71
    C. 95
    D. 114
    E. 151

49. A student wants to find information on a church built in 1518. On which of the following pages should the student begin to look for this information?
    A. 59
    B. 105
    C. 107
    D. 153
    E. 179

Use the following excerpt for question 50.

    I.   **Types of Teas**

        A. Black Tea

            1) Assam

            2) Darjeeling

            3) Ceylon

        B. _____

        C. White Tea

50. Based on the pattern in the headings, which of the following is a reasonable heading to insert in the blank spot?
   A.   Green Tea
   B.   Iced Tea
   C.   Cold-Brew Tea
   D.   Chai Tea
   E.   Oolong Tea

Mathematics

Work the problem, and then choose the most correct answer.

1. The population of a town was 7250 in 2014 and 7375 in 2015. What was the percent increase from 2014 to 2015 to the nearest tenth of a percent?
   A.   1.5%
   B.   1.6%
   C.   1.7%
   D.   1.8%
   E.   2.0%

2. Which of the following numbers are equivalent to 2.61?
   A.   2.601
   B. $\frac{261}{10}$
   C.   2.061
   D. $\frac{261}{100}$
   E. $\frac{261}{1000}$

3. The line of best fit is calculated for a data set that tracks the number of miles that passenger cars traveled annually in the US from 1960 to 2010. In the model, $x = 0$ represents the year 1960, and y is the number of miles traveled in billions. If the line of best fit is $y = 0.0293x + 0.563$, approximately how many additional miles were traveled for every 5 years that passed?
   A.   0.0293 billion
   B.   0.1465 billion
   C.   0.5630 billion
   D.   0.7100 billion
   E.   2.9615 billion

4. Which number has the greatest value?
   A.   9299 ones
   B.   903 tens
   C.   93 hundreds
   D.   9 thousands
   E.   9 thousandths

5. If a car uses 8 gallons of gas to travel 650 miles, how many miles can it travel using 12 gallons of gas?
   A.   870 miles
   B.   895 miles
   C.   915 miles
   D.   975 miles
   E.   1025 miles

6. Rectangular water tank A is 5 feet long, 10 feet wide, and 4 feet tall. Rectangular tank B is 5 feet long, 5 feet wide, and 4 feet tall. If the same amount of water is poured into both tanks and the height of the water in tank A is 1 foot, how high will the water be in tank B?
   A.   1 foot
   B.   2 feet
   C.   3 feet
   D.   4 feet
   E.   5 feet

7. The graph below shows the number of months that Chicago, New York, and Houston had less than 3 inches of rain from 2009 to 2015.

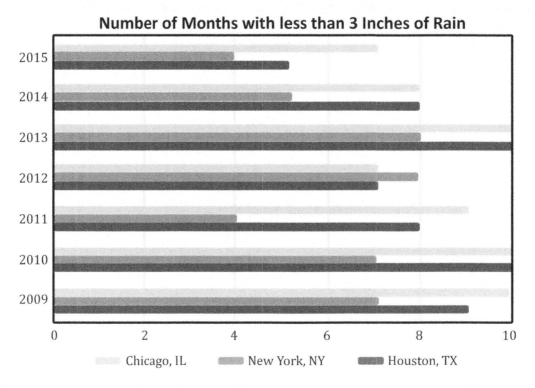

From 2009 to 2015, what is the average number of months that Chicago had less than 3 inches of rain?
- A. 5
- B. 6
- C. 7
- D. 8
- E. 9

8. In the sequence below, each term is found by finding the difference between the previous two numbers and multiplying the result by −3. What is the 6th term of the sequence?

$$\{3, 0, 9, -27, \dots\}$$

- A. −405
- B. −135
- C. 45
- D. 81
- E. 135

9. The ratio of nurses to doctors in a hospital unit is 3:1. Which of the following could be the total number of nurses and doctors in the unit?
- A. 28
- B. 30
- C. 31
- D. 34
- E. 38

10. The figure below shows a rectangle with 4 square cutouts made to each corner. What is the area of the resulting shape?

   A.   142 cm^2
   B.   200 cm^2
   C.   296 cm^2
   D.   320 cm^2
   E.   492 cm^2

11. A group of 20 friends is planning a road trip. They have 3 cars that seat 4 people, 3 cars that seat 5 people, and 1 car that seats 6 people. What is the fewest number of cars they can take on the trip if each person needs his or her own seat?
   A.   3 cars
   B.   4 cars
   C.   5 cars
   D.   6 cars
   E.   7 cars

12. Solve the following equation for y: $3(2y + 1) + 3 = 4(y - 2)$
   A.   −7
   B.   −6
   C.   −1
   D.   7
   E.   14

13. If a student answers 129 out of 150 questions correctly on a quiz, what percentage of questions did she answer incorrectly?
   A.   10%
   B.   12%
   C.   14%
   D.   15%
   E.   17%

14. Solve the following equation for x: $6x - 7 = 5(2x + 1)$
   A.   −3
   B.   −2
   C.   3
   D.   4
   E.   5

15. The formula for distance is $d = v \times t$, where v is the object's velocity and t is the time. How long will it take a plane to fly 4000 miles from Chicago to London if the plane flies at a constant rate of 500 mph?
   A.   0.125 hours
   B.   3.5 hours
   C.   8 hours
   D.   20 hours
   E.   45 hours

16. If $4x = 3$, what is the value of $8x$?
   A.   0.75
   B.   6
   C.   12
   D.   24
   E.   32

17. A semicircle is drawn next to the base of an isosceles triangle such that its diameter is perpendicular to the triangle's altitude. What is the area of the resulting figure shown below?

6 cm

10 cm

   A.   30
   B. $30 + 4.5\pi$
   C. $30 + 9\pi$
   D. $30 + 36\pi$
   E. $60 + 4.5\pi$

18. Justin has a summer lawn care business and earns $40 for each lawn he mows. He also pays $35 per week in business expenses. Which of the following expressions represents Justin's profit after x weeks if he mows m number of lawns?
   A. $40m - 35x$
   B. $40m + 35x$
   C. $35x(40 + m)$
   D. $35(40m + x)$
   E. $40x(35 + m)$

19. An ice chest contains 24 sodas, some regular and some diet. The ratio of diet soda to regular soda is 1:3. How many regular sodas are there in the ice chest?
    A. 1
    B. 4
    C. 6
    D. 18
    E. 24

20. At the grocery store, apples cost $1.89 per pound and oranges cost $2.19 per pound. How much would it cost to purchase 2 pounds of apples and 1.5 pounds of oranges?
    A. $6.62
    B. $7.07
    C. $7.14
    D. $7.22
    E. $7.67

21. Which of the following sequences follows the same rule as the sequence below?

$$30, 27, 24, 21, \ldots$$

    A. 41, 39, 37, 35,...
    B. 41, 44, 47, 50,...
    C. 41, 37, 33, 29,...
    D. 41, 38, 35, 32,...
    E. 41, 27, 24, 21,...

22. A car traveled at 65 miles per hour for $1\frac{1}{2}$ hours and then traveled at 50 miles per hour for $2\frac{1}{2}$ hours. How many miles did the car travel?
    A. 115 miles
    B. 200 miles
    C. 222.5 miles
    D. 237.5 miles
    E. 260 miles

23. In the figure below, triangles ABF and CDE are equilateral. If the perimeter of the figure is 60 inches, what is the area of square BCEF in square inches?

    A.   60
    B.   100
    C.   120
    D.   140
    E.   144

24. If $5x + 2 = 2y$ and $y = 6$, what is the value of x?
    A.   2
    B.   3
    C.   4
    D.   5
    E.   6

25. Points W, X, Y, and Z lie on a circle with center A. If the diameter of the circle is 75, what is the sum of AW, AX, AY, and AZ?
    A.   75
    B.   100
    C.   125
    D.   300
    E.   150

26. Adam is painting the outside of a four-walled shed. The shed is 5 feet wide, 4 feet deep, and 7 feet high. How many square feet of paint will Adam need to paint the four sides of the shed?
    A.   80
    B.   126
    C.   140
    D.   252
    E.   560

27. If the volume of a cube is 343 cubic meters, what is the cube's surface area?
    A. $49 \, m^2$
    B. $84 \, m^2$
    C. $196 \, m^2$
    D. $294 \, m^2$
    E. $343 \, m^2$

28. The mean of 13 numbers is 30. If the mean of 8 of these numbers is 42, what is the mean of the other 5 numbers?
   A.   5.5
   B.   10.8
   C.   16.4
   D.   21.2
   E.   30.0

29. Kendrick has $2,386.52 in his checking account. If he pays $792.00 for rent, $84.63 for groceries, and $112.15 for his car insurance, how much money will he have left in his account?
   A. $1,397.74
   B. $1,482.37
   C. $1,509.89
   D. $2,189.22
   E. $3,375.30

30. In the fall, 425 students pass the math benchmark. In the spring, 680 students pass the same benchmark. What is the percentage increase in passing scores from fall to spring?
   A.   37.5%
   B.   55%
   C.   60%
   D.   62.5%
   E.   80%

31. If one serving of milk contains 280 milligrams of calcium, how much calcium is in 1.5 servings?
   A.   187 mg
   B.   200 mg
   C.   295 mg
   D.   420 mg
   E.   560 mg

32. What number is in the hundredths place when 21.563 is divided by 8?
   A.   3
   B.   5
   C.   6
   D.   7
   E.   9

33. Which of the following operations is equivalent to dividing by 100?
   A.   multiplying by $\frac{1}{100}$

   B.   adding −100

   C.   dividing by $\frac{1}{100}$

   D.   subtracting 100

   E.   multiplying by 0.001

34. Which of the following is equivalent to the term $5n$ for all values of n?

    A. $5n^5 - n^4$

    B. $3n + 2n$

    C. n^5

    D. $5 + n$

    E. $5n \times n$

35. Which of the following numbers is between $5\frac{1}{4}$ and $5\frac{1}{2}$?

    A. $5\frac{5}{8}$

    B. $5\frac{7}{20}$

    C. $5\frac{3}{4}$

    D. $5\frac{1}{10}$

    E. $5\frac{8}{15}$

36. What is the median of all the even integers greater than 10 and less than 25?

    A. 12

    B. 14

    C. 16

    D. 18

    E. 20

37. A fifth-grade teacher has her class check a rain gauge every day for five days. The students then draw their data on a graph as shown below.

What was the average daily rainfall over the five days?

    A. 0.45 inches

    B. 0.5 inches

    C. 0.65 inches

    D. 0.75 inches

    E. 1.25 inches

38. A 10 L container will hold how much more liquid than a 2 gallon container? ($1\ gal = 3.785\ L$)
   A. 2.00 L
   B. 2.43 L
   C. 6.22 L
   D. 8.00 L
   E. 9.47 L

39. A cyclist is moving down the sidewalk at 15 feet per second. What is his approximate speed in miles per hour?
   A. 10.2 mph
   B. 15.9 mph
   C. 17.1 mph
   D. 22 mph
   E. 30.7 mph

40. If ABCD is a rectangle, which of the following statements must be true?

   A. $\angle AQD \cong \angle AQB$

   B. $AB \cong AD$

   C. $\triangle AQD \cong \triangle BQC$

   D. $m\angle AQB = 90^\circ$

   E. $AB = 2(AD)$

41. In the Venn diagram below, set A includes all the factors of 24, and set B includes all the factors of 28. What is the probability that a number selected at random from the shaded region will be 2?

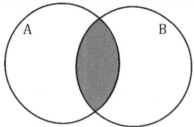

A. $\frac{1}{4}$

B. $\frac{1}{3}$

C. $\frac{1}{2}$

D. $\frac{2}{3}$

E. $\frac{3}{4}$

42. Melissa is ordering fencing to enclose a square area of 5,625 square feet. Which of the following is the number of feet of fencing she needs?
   A.   75
   B.   150
   C.   300
   D.   1,405
   E.   5,625

43. A circular swimming pool has a circumference of 50 feet. Which of the following is the diameter of the pool in feet?
   A) 25π

   B) $\frac{25}{\pi}$

   C) 50π

   D) $\frac{50}{\pi}$

   E) $50\pi + 25$

44. The pie graph below shows how a state's government plans to spend its annual budget of $3 billion. How much more money does the state plan to spend on infrastructure than education?

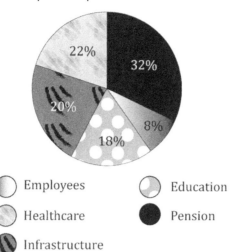

⬤ Employees   ◐ Education

◓ Healthcare   ⬤ Pension

◉ Infrastructure

    A. $60,000,000
    B. $120,000,000
    C. $300,000,000
    D. $540,000,000
    E. $600,000,000

45. The perimeter of a rectangle is 42 millimeters. If the length of the rectangle is 13 millimeters, what is its width in millimeters?
    A.   6
    B.   7
    C.   8
    D.   12
    E.   13

46. Robbie has a bag of treats that contains 5 pieces of gum, 7 pieces of taffy, and 8 pieces of chocolate. If Robbie reaches into the bag and randomly pulls out a treat, what is the probability that Robbie will get a piece of taffy?
    A. $\frac{1}{13}$

    B. $\frac{1}{7}$

    C. $\frac{7}{20}$

    D. $\frac{7}{13}$

    E. $\frac{13}{20}$

47. What is the remainder when 397 is divided by 4?

  A. 0
  B. 1
  C. 2
  D. 3
  E. 4

48. Which of the following symbols should be placed in the box to form a true statement?

$$-\frac{3}{4} \quad \square \quad -\frac{1}{2}$$

  A. >
  B. <
  C. ≥
  D. ≤
  E. =

49. Solve the following inequality for x: $6x + 5 \geq -15 + 8x$?

  A. $x \geq 5$
  B. $x \leq 5$
  C. $x \geq 10$
  D. $x \leq 10$
  E. $x \leq 20$

50. A patient was administered pain medication at 11:30 p.m. The patient can have another dose in 4.5 hours. At what time can the patient have another dose?

  A. 3:30 a.m.
  B. 4:00 a.m.
  C. 4:30 a.m.
  D. 4:00 p.m.
  E. 4:30 p.m.

Writing

Read the prompt, and then write a short essay defending your opinion.

Topic 1

1. Since almost every industry in the world depends on oil and gas extraction, many argue that it is vital that companies be allowed to use whatever methods necessary to continue supplying the world with this resource—even practices like fracking that pollute sensitive ecosystems.

State whether you agree or disagree with this opinion, and support your position with logical arguments and specific examples.

> State whether you agree or disagree with this opinion, and support your position with logical arguments and specific examples

Topic 2

2. Rapid population growth has not permitted adequate urban planning in areas prone to extreme weather, and the proliferation of slums means that more lives will be lost in the case of storms or floods. If slowing urban growth means limiting economic growth, so be it: the risks of flooding from unpredictable and violent climate patterns are too great.

> State whether you agree or disagree with this opinion, and support your position with logical arguments and specific examples.

The next few pages are blank for you to write your essay.

Answer Key #1

Reading

1. B: The author writes that "[j]azz music was played by and for a more expressive and freed populace than the United States had previously seen." In addition to "the emergence of the flapper," the 1920s saw "the explosion of African American art and culture now known as the Harlem Renaissance."

2. A: The author writes that "[j]azz music was played by and for a more expressive and freed populace than the United States had previously seen." In addition to "the emergence of the flapper," the 1920s saw "the explosion of African American art and culture now known as the Harlem Renaissance."

3. C: The author opens the passage saying, "In recent decades, jazz has been associated with New Orleans and festivals like Mardi Gras, but in the 1920s, jazz was a booming trend whose influence reached into many aspects of American culture." He then goes on to elaborate on what these movements were.

4. B: At the end of the first paragraph, the author writes, "Ella Fitzgerald, for example, moved from Virginia to New York City to begin her much-lauded singing career, and jazz pioneer Louis Armstrong got his big break in Chicago."

5. C: The author writes that "[j]azz music was played by and for a more expressive and freed populace than the United States had previously seen." In addition to "the emergence of the flapper," the 1920s saw "the explosion of African American art and culture now known as the Harlem Renaissance."

6. D: The passage gives a short history of thermonuclear weapons and then introduces its main topic—the physical and biological consequences of nuclear war.

7. D: The word "given" best describes the idea that the gifts have been handed out: "to the lion [Epimetheus] gave strength; to the bird, swiftness; to the fox, sagacity; and so on."

8. B: The author states that the South's explanations for the war are "fanciful inventions" designed to cover up history, implying these explanations are imaginative or false.

9. A: The author writes, "But people who try to sell you this narrative are wrong. The Civil War was not a battle of cultural identities—it was a battle about slavery."

10. B: The author writes, "The Civil War was not a battle of cultural identities—it was a battle about slavery. All other explanations for the war are either a direct consequence of the South's desire for wealth at the expense of her fellow man or a fanciful invention to cover up this sad portion of our nation's history."

11. B: The author says that the house on Pine Street "had enough space inside but didn't have a big enough yard for [their] three dogs."

12. A: The author argues that "every man, woman, and child should learn" to swim, and then explains to the reader why he or she should be able to swim.

13. B: In February the service earned $1,100, and in April it earned $200. The difference between the two months is $900.

14. B: The author uses several markers of casual writing, including the first person, exclamation marks, and informal language.

15. A: This detail is not stated in the passage.

16. B: In the first paragraph, the author writes, "But what's the best way to get an accurate reading? The answer depends on the situation." She then goes on to describe various options and their applications.

17. B: The author indicates that "[t]he most common way people measure body temperature is orally" but that "[t]here are many situations…when measuring temperature orally isn't an option." She then goes on to describe these situations in the second and third paragraphs.

18. A: The final paragraph states that "agitated patients…won't be able to sit still long enough for an accurate reading." The reader can infer that an agitated patient is a patient who is visibly upset, annoyed, or uncomfortable.

19. A: The second paragraph of the passage states that "[u]sing the rectum also has the added benefit of providing a much more accurate reading than other locations can provide."

20. D: The author writes, "The army set high standards: all of the recruits had to be skilled on horseback."

21. A: The author states that "[p]opcorn continued to rule the snack food kingdom until the rise in popularity of home televisions during the 1950s" when the industry saw a "decline in sales" as a result of the changing pastimes of the American people.

22. B: The author states, "For the Aztec Indians who called the caves home, popcorn (or *momochitl*) played an important role in society, both as a food staple and in ceremonies." This implies that the Aztec people popped popcorn both for special occasions ("in ceremonies") and for regular consumption ("as a food staple").

23. C: In the opening paragraph the author writes, "But popcorn isn't just for fun— it's also a multimillion-dollar-a-year industry with a long and fascinating history." The author then goes on to illustrate the history of popcorn from the ancient Aztecs, to early twentieth-century America, to the present day.

24. C: The author writes, "The popcorn industry flourished during the Great Depression when it was advertised as a wholesome and economical food."

25. A: This statement summarizes the entire passage, including the brief history of popcorn in ancient cultures and the growth in the popularity of popcorn in America.

26. C: The author writes, "However, it wasn't until microwave popcorn became commercially available in 1981 that at-home popcorn consumption began to grow exponentially. With the wide availability of microwaves in the United States, popcorn also began popping up in offices and hotel rooms."

27. D: The author writes, "*The Scream of Nature* by Edvard Munch is one of the world's best known and most desirable artworks."

28. D: The passage describes human studies as the study of "the relationship between human activity and the environment," which would include farmers interacting with river systems.

29. A: The passage explains what the study of geography involves and outlines its main subdisciplines.

Answer Key #1

30. B: Only this choice summarizes the two main points of the passage: the definition of geography and the breakdown of its subdisciplines.

31. A: The author goes on to describe the shared perspectives of these writers.

32. B: The author writes that "a number of myths about animal pain still plague the field of veterinary medicine and prevent practitioners from making pain management a priority."

33. D: The author writes that "[e]ven the emotional reaction to a painful experience, like being afraid to return to the dentist after an unpleasant visit, is mirrored in animals."

34. A: The author writes that animals mask pain in response to the "<u>foreign</u> environment of a veterinary office," implying that the office is unfamiliar to the animal.

35. D: The author writes, "Although many advancements have been made in research sciences...a number of myths about animal pain still plague the field of veterinary medicine and prevent practitioners from making pain management a priority."

36. B: The author writes that "veterinarians must be aware of the survival instinct of many animals to mask pain in response to stressful experiences or foreign environments. For these reasons, diagnostic tools and strategies are instrumental in the effective practice of veterinary medicine."

37. D: The author writes that to diagnose pain in animals, "a veterinarian might make use of an objective pain scale, by which he or she could assess the animal's condition according to a number of criteria. This tool is especially useful throughout the course of treatment, as it provides the practitioner with a quantitative measure for evaluating the effectiveness of various treatment options."

38. C: The author of Passage 1 indicates that "according to Grant, the biological mechanisms by which we experience pain are the very same mechanisms by which animals experience pain." This indicates that the author believes that pain and the process of pain management are somewhat similar in animals and humans.

39. B: The author of the first passage writes that "a number of myths about animal pain still plague the field of veterinary medicine and prevent practitioners from making pain management a priority." This implies that the author believes pain management should be a priority of veterinarians. The second author writes that "diagnostic tools and strategies are instrumental in the effective practice of veterinary medicine" and then goes on to describe some of these tools.

40. A: The first author writes, "Grant emphasizes that veterinarians must be aware that a lack of obvious signs does not necessarily suggest that pain is not present: in fact, many animals, especially those that are prey animals in the wild, are likely to conceal their pain out of an instinct to hide weaknesses that may make them easy targets for predators." The second author agrees, saying that "veterinarians must be aware of the survival instinct of many animals to mask pain in response to stressful experiences or foreign environments."

41. A: Twenty-five students earned an F in science, and 70 students earned an A in science; $2(25) < 70$.

42. C: The author describes a situation in which civil disobedience had an enormous impact.

43. B: The paragraph states that "[f]lags are everywhere"; from context, the reader should understand that they are visible at government buildings.

44. C: The passage discusses the many kinds of flags, and notes that the FIAV was formed to help keep track of the increase in flags with the decolonization movements in the 1960s.

45. A: It is reasonable to assume that many countries becoming independent around the same time would result in a glut of new flags, and an organization like the FIAV would help keep track of them and avoid problems like duplication of design.

46. B: The author states, "Ignored by the government, an activist group known as Indians of All Tribes sailed to Alcatraz in the early morning hours with eighty-nine men, women, and children." The author goes on to describe the nineteen-month occupation of the island.

47. C: The author presents the reasons for the debate and both sides of the argument.

48. A: Page 55 is included in the section about Italian painters.

49. D: Page 153 is the beginning of the section on High Renaissance architecture, which includes the year 1518.

50. A: Only the heading *Green Tea* fits the pattern of headings that describe categories of tea based on color.

Mathematics

1. C: Use the formula for percent change.

$$percent\ change = \frac{amount\ of\ change}{original\ amount} = \frac{7375 - 7250}{7250} = 0.017 = \mathbf{1.7\%}$$

2. D: Dividing 261 by 100 will move the decimal two places to the left:

$$\frac{261}{100} = \mathbf{2.61}$$

3. B: The slope 0.0293 gives the increase in passenger car miles (in billions) for each year that passes. Multiply this value by 5 to find the increase that occurs over 5 years:

$$5(0.0293) = \mathbf{0.1465\ billion\ miles}$$

4. C: Write out each number to find the largest.

    A. $9299\ ones\ = 9299$

    B. $903\ tens\ = 9030$

    C. $\mathbf{93\ hundreds\ = 9300}$

    D. $9\ thousands\ = 9000$

    E. $9\ thousandths\ = 0.009$

5. D: Set up a proportion and solve.

$$\frac{8}{650} = \frac{12}{x}$$

$$8x = (650)(12)$$

$$x = \mathbf{975\ miles}$$

6. B: Calculate the volume of water in tank A.

$$V = l \times w \times h$$

$$5 \times 10 \times 1 = 50\ ft^3$$

Find the height this volume would reach in tank B.

$$V = l \times w \times h$$

$$50 = 5 \times 5 \times h$$

$$h = \mathbf{2\ ft}$$

7. E: Use the graph to find the number of months Chicago had less than 3 inches of rain year, and then find the average.

Months with < 3 inches of rain in Chicago:

$$\{7, 8, 10, 7, 9, 10, 10\}$$

$$\frac{7 + 8 + 10 + 7 + 9 + 10 + 10}{7} = 8.7 \approx \mathbf{9}$$

8. A: Find the 5th term.

$$-27 - 9 = -36$$

$$-36 \times -3 = 108$$

Find the 6th term.

$$108 - (-27) = 135$$

$$135 \times -3 = \mathbf{-405}$$

9. A: If the ratio of nurses to doctors is $3 : 1$, then the total number of nurses and doctors must be a multiple of 4 (because $3 + 1$).

10. D: Find the area of the complete rectangle and subtract the area of the missing corners.

rectangle:

$$A = lw = (20 + 2 + 2) \times (10 + 2 + 2) = 336\ cm^2$$

corners:

$$A = 4(lw) = 4(2 \times 2) = 16 \ cm^2$$

$$336 - 16 = \mathbf{320 \ cm^2}$$

11. B: Using the cars with the largest capacity first, add together the seats in the cars until there are 20.

$$6 + 5 = 11$$

$$6 + 5 + 5 = 16$$

$$6 + 5 + 5 + 5 = 21$$

The fewest number of cars that will seat 20 people is **4 cars.**

12. A:

$$3(2y + 1) + 3 = 4(y - 2)$$

$$6y + 3 + 3 = 4y - 8$$

$$6y + 6 = 4y - 8$$

$$6y = 4y - 14$$

$$2y = -14$$

$$\mathbf{y = -7}$$

13. C: Subtract to find the number of questions the student answered incorrectly.

$$150 - 129 = 21$$

Use the formula for percentages.

$$percent = \frac{part}{whole} = \frac{21}{150} = 0.14 = \mathbf{14\%}$$

14. A: Solve for x by isolating the variable on one side of the equation.

$$6x - 7 = 5(2x + 1)$$

$$6x - 7 = 10x + 5$$

$$6x = 10x + 12$$

$$-4x = 12$$

$$\mathbf{x = -3}$$

15. C: Plug the given values into the equation and solve for t.

$$d = v \times t$$

$$4000 = 500 \times t$$

$$t = \mathbf{8 \ hours}$$

16. B: Multiply each side by 2.

$$4x = 3$$
$$2(4x) = 2(3)$$
$$8x = 6$$

17. B: Add the area of the semicircle and the area of the triangle.

semicircle:

$$A = \frac{\pi r^2}{2} = \frac{\pi (3)^2}{2} = 4.5\pi$$

triangle:

$$A = \frac{1}{2}bh = \frac{1}{2}(6)(10) = 30$$

total area:

$$30 + 4.5\pi$$

18. A: Justin's profit will be his income minus his expenses. He will earn $40 for each lawn, or 40m. He pays $35 in expenses each week, or $35x$.

$$\text{profit} = 40m - 35x$$

19. D: Solve the problem using a proportion. The ratio of diet to regular is $1:3$, so the total number of sodas is a multiple of 4.

$$\frac{3}{4} = \frac{x}{24}$$
$$4x = 3(24)$$
$$4x = 72$$
$$x = 18$$

20. B: Multiply the cost per pound by the number of pounds purchased to find the cost of each fruit.

apples:

$$2(1.89) = 3.78$$

oranges:

$$1.5(2.19) = 3.285$$
$$3.78 + 3.285 = 7.065 = \$7.07$$

21. D: The given sequence is formed by subtracting 3 from the previous value in the sequence.

22. C: Multiply the car's speed by the time traveled to find the distance.

$$1.5(65) = 97.5 \ miles$$

$$2.5(50) = 125 \ miles$$

$$97.5 + 125 = \boldsymbol{222.5 \ miles}$$

23. B: The sides in equilateral triangles are all the same length, and the sides of a square are all the same length. Because the triangles and the square share a side, all the lines in the figure are the same length. The perimeter can be used to find the length of one side:

$$60 \ inches \div 6 = 10 \ inches$$

Multiply two sides of the square to find its area:

$$10 \ in \times 10 \ in = \boldsymbol{100 \ in^2}$$

24. A: Plug in the given value for y and solve for x.

$$5x + 2 = 2y$$

$$5x + 2 = 2(6)$$

$$5x + 2 = 12$$

$$5x + 2 - 2 = 12 - 2$$

$$5x = 10$$

$$\frac{5x}{5} = \frac{10}{5}$$

$$\boldsymbol{x = 2}$$

25. E: All the points lie on the circle, so each line segment is a radius. The sum of the 4 lines will be 4 times the radius.

$$r = \frac{75}{2} = 37.5$$

$$4r = \boldsymbol{150}$$

26. B: Find the area of all sides of the shed. Two walls measure 5 feet by 7 feet; the other two walls measure 4 feet by 7 feet.

$$A = 2l_1 w_1 + 2l_2 w_2$$

$$A = 2(5 \ ft)(7 \ ft) + 2(4 \ ft)(7 \ ft)$$

$$A = 70 \ ft^2 + 56 \ ft^2 = 126 \ ft^2$$

27. D: Use the volume to find the length of the cube's side.

$$V = s^3$$

$$343 = s^3$$

$$s = 7\,m$$

Find the area of each side.

$$7(7) = 49\,m^2$$

Multiply the area of each side by 6 to find the total surface area.

$$49(6) = \mathbf{294\,m^2}$$

28. B: Find the sum of the 13 numbers whose mean is 30.

$$13 \times 30 = 390$$

Find the sum of the 8 numbers whose mean is 42.

$$8 \times 42 = 336$$

Find the sum and mean of the remaining 5 numbers.

$$390 - 336 = 54$$

$$\frac{54}{5} = \mathbf{10.8}$$

29. A: Subtract the amount of the bills from the amount in the checking account.

$$792.00 + 84.63 + 112.15 = 988.78$$

$$2386.52 - 988.78 = \mathbf{\$1397.74}$$

30. C: Use the formula for percent change.

$$percent\ change = \frac{amount\ of\ change}{original\ amount} = \frac{680 - 425}{425} = 0.6 = \mathbf{60\%}$$

31. D: Set up a proportion and solve.

$$\frac{1}{280} = \frac{1.5}{x}$$

$$x = (280)(1.5)$$

$$x = \mathbf{420}$$

32. E: Divide and find the digit in the hundredths place.

$$21.563 \div 8 = \mathbf{2.695375}$$

33. A: Dividing by 100 produces the same result as multiplying by $\frac{1}{100}$.

$$n \div 100 = \frac{n}{100}$$

$$n \times \frac{1}{100} = \frac{n}{100}$$

34. B: Combine like terms.

$$3n + 2n = 5n$$

35. B: Convert each fraction in the problem to a decimal.

$$5\frac{1}{4} = 5.25$$

$$5\frac{1}{2} = 5.5$$

Convert each answer choice to a decimal, and find the value between 5.25 and 5.5.

A: $5\frac{5}{8} = 5.625$

B: $5\frac{7}{20} = \mathbf{5.35}$

C: $5\frac{3}{4} = 5.75$

D: $5\frac{1}{10} = 5.1$

E: $5\frac{8}{15} = 5.533$

36. D: List all the even integers greater than 10 and less than 25 in ascending order. The median is the value in the middle.

$$12, 14, 16, \mathbf{18}, 20, 22, 24$$

37. C: To find the average, add the rainfall amounts and divide by 5.

$$\frac{0.75 + 1.25 + 0 + 0.5 + 0.75}{5} = \mathbf{0.65\ inches}$$

38. B: The answer choices are in liters, so convert gallons to liters.

$$2\ gal \times \frac{3.785\ L}{1\ gal} = 7.57\ L$$

Subtract to find the difference in liters.

$$10\ L - 7.57\ L = \mathbf{2.43\ L}$$

39. A: Use dimensional analysis to convert feet to miles and seconds to hours.

$$\frac{15 \ ft}{1 \ sec} \times \frac{3600 \ sec}{1 \ hr} \times \frac{1 \ mi}{5280 \ ft} \approx \mathbf{10.2 \ mph}$$

40. C: The diagonals of a rectangle create two sets of congruent triangles.

41. B: Find all the numbers in the shaded region by identifying the factors of 24 and 28.

$$24: 1, 2, 3, 4, 6, 8, 12, 24$$

$$28: 1, 2, 4, 7, 14, 28$$

The set of numbers in the shaded region is $\{1, 2, 4\}$, so the total number of possible outcomes is 3.

Use the formula for probability.

$$P(selecting \ 2) = \frac{number \ of \ favorable \ outcomes}{total \ number \ of \ possible \ outcomes} = \frac{1}{3}$$

42. C: Use the area to find the length of one side of the square.

$$A = s^2$$

$$5,625 = s^2$$

$$\sqrt{5,625} = s$$

$$s = 75 \ ft$$

Now multiply the side length by 4 to find the perimeter.

$$P = 4s$$

$$P = 4(75 \ ft.) = \mathbf{300 \ ft}$$

43. D: The formula for the circumference of a circle is $C = 2\pi r$.

Because $d = 2r$, this formula can be rewritten:

$$C = \pi d$$

$$50 \ ft = \pi d$$

$$d = \frac{50}{\pi}$$

44. A: Find the amount the state will spend on infrastructure and education, and then find the difference.

$$infrastructure = 0.2(3,000,000,000) = 600,000,000$$

$$education = 0.18(3,000,000,000) = 540,000,000$$

$$600,000,000 - 540,000,000 = \mathbf{\$60,000,000}$$

45. C: Use the equation for the perimeter of a rectangle.

$$P = 2l + 2w$$
$$42 = 2(13) + 2w$$
$$\mathbf{w = 8}$$

46. C: Use the equation for probability.

$$P(an\ event) = \frac{number\ of\ favorable\ outcomes}{total\ number\ of\ possible\ outcomes}$$

$$P = \frac{7}{5 + 7 + 8} = \frac{\mathbf{7}}{\mathbf{20}}$$

47. B: Find the highest possible multiple of 4 that is less than or equal to 397, and then subtract to find the remainder.

$$99 \times 4 = 396$$
$$397 - 396 = \mathbf{1}$$

48. B: $-\frac{3}{4}$ is less than $-\frac{1}{2}$.

49. D: Isolate the variable on the left side of the inequality. Reverse the direction of the inequality when dividing by a negative number.

$$6x + 5 \geq -15 + 8x$$
$$-2x + 5 \geq -15$$
$$-2x \geq -20$$
$$\mathbf{x \leq 10}$$

50. B: 4.5 hours after 11:30 p.m. is **4:00 a.m.**

Writing

Essay One

To be sure, extracting petroleum and natural gas requires hard choices and results in environmental damage. Around the world, oil and gas are obtained through drilling in deserts, off deep-sea platforms, and now, through fracking, which can damage the earth and water resources. However, fossil fuels are essential to industry and the global economy. Oil and gas make it possible for the world to use electricity and transportation. Furthermore, the economic fate of millions is directly tied to the fossil fuels industry; the livelihoods of workers around the world, from roughnecks to office staff, depend on the oil and gas market. While oil and gas extraction can have negative consequences for the environment, it is too important to the global economy to limit exploration and production.

While the oil and gas prices rise and fall, and the market can be unpredictable, there will be demand for fossil fuels for years to come. Rapidly growing countries like China, whose populations are beginning to demand products like automobiles, will require more petroleum than ever. Despite efforts to conserve energy and protect the environment, industrial production continues worldwide, including in countries with limited environmental protection laws in the developing world. Furthermore, international organizations like the World Trade Organization allow major corporations to sue countries in order to weaken environmental protection laws in favor of production. Fossil fuels power not only consumer goods like cars, but large-scale industrial production as well. Alternative sources of energy (like wind and solar power) do exist, but not on the same scale as oil and gas.

In addition, several countries located in oil-producing regions have become wealthy and powerful thanks to this natural resource. Saudi Arabia, Kuwait, the United Arab Emirates, Russia, Nigeria, Angola, Iran, and Iraq are a few examples of major oil producers. Given the importance of oil to the world economy, the wealth of these countries helps make them important voices in regional and international affairs; furthermore, oil wealth gives them the ability to form strategic alliances with world powers. It is unlikely that major oil producers would give up their substantial geostrategic power in favor of environmental protection.

In an ideal world, the global economy would flourish while the environment did the same. However, in order to make the most of natural resources, sacrifices are required. Perhaps environmental activism and new technology can help the world community find a way forward in order to safely extract the resources the world economy needs, and improve energy efficiency to make the most of those resources we already have.

Essay Two

Violent storms are a huge risk to human life and property; they also have a strong impact on the economy, interfering with economic activity and sometimes damaging infrastructure. However, natural disasters are a fact of life on our planet, and it is impossible for economic development and growth to cease due to the possibility of a powerful storm. Still, rapid urban development is occurring in particularly storm-prone areas in Asia and even in North America, putting millions of people at risk. While the risks of a calamitous storm should never be underestimated, the solution is not to halt migration and slow economic growth, but to encourage investment in urban planning and public safety.

Centers of population in storm-prone areas in Indonesia, the Philippines, the United States East and Gulf Coasts, and elsewhere are indeed growing; natural resources and urban areas in these places are essential to local and national economies and even the global economy. During this time of change, especially in areas that are newly developing, opportunities for proper urban planning abound. Before growing urban areas get even larger, governments must take action to prevent the proliferation of slums, improve existing infrastructure to meet the needs of growing cities (or develop new infrastructure), and put policies into place for good urban management. Given the importance of these urban and industrial areas, especially for billion-dollar sectors like the oil and gas industry, there may even be opportunities for major companies to get involved in sponsoring urban development and safety in the economic zones and cities relevant to their interests around the world.

Furthermore, with economic growth also comes innovation and technology. Today, there are more opportunities than ever to develop products and procedures to ensure safety. From engineering to preparedness to emergency medical treatment, there are a plethora of approaches to storm readiness and flood control. Urban planning can take into account flooding and geographical impediments to emergency response time. There are more products on the market to help families survive for several days without help (for instance, water purifiers and generators). Governments, civic organizations, and NGOs could be involved in emergency preparedness efforts and enlisted to distribute preparedness items during storm seasons, especially to those poor and working people who are the most likely to be affected and who, according to the passage, would most likely be harmed. Using good technology and wise community coordination would ensure that vulnerable workers and their families are as safe as possible during storm season, so that they could benefit year-round from economic growth.

While storms and other natural disasters are and will remain a threat to human life, it is unrealistic to imagine that all economic activity will stop for the sake of safety. Thanks to economic growth and innovation, we can develop planning, technology, policy, and coordination to ensure the safety of communities as they drive the economic growth of those regions affected by major storms. That way, development can continue in as safe an environment as possible.

Practice Test #2

Reading

Use the following passage for questions 1 – 3.

Communicating with any human being in crisis—whether that crisis is physical or emotional—is going to be more difficult than normal, everyday communication. Thus, emergency responders and medical practitioners, like many other social service providers, need to learn how to be sensitive in interpersonal communication. Here are some tips about how to hone your craft as a communicator while working with people in crisis. These tips can also be used for everyday communication.

First, it is essential that you are aware of cultural differences. In some cultures, direct eye contact can be unsettling or disrespectful. People from different cultures may have different comfort levels with personal space: some might find physical closeness comforting; others might find it threatening. Your body language speaks volumes. Be sure you are aware of the symbolic nature of your posture, hand motions, and gestures.

It is also important to enunciate your verbal statements and directions in a clear, relevant way. Use terminology and directions that a patient will understand, and avoid lofty medical jargon. Believe it or not, you also want to be honest with the person in crisis, even if the conditions are dire. Also explain, if possible, what you might do to help alleviate even the most drastic conditions so that the person feels supported. Lastly, and most importantly, be prepared to listen. Even if there is a language barrier, condition, or disability limiting your communication with the person in crisis, try to position yourself as an active listener. These tips will help you support people who need clarity and sensitivity.

1). What is the best summary of the passage?
   A.   In some cultures, direct eye contact can be unsettling or disrespectful.
   B.   Posture, hand motions, and gestures can symbolize respect or disrespect.
   C.   Medical practitioners must learn to be sensitive with people who are in crisis.
   D.   Medical practitioners should give clear directions and avoid using lofty medical jargon.
   E.   It is always best practice to be honest with people who are in crisis.

2). What is the author's primary purpose for writing this essay?
   A.   to warn people about the dangers of disrespectful communication
   B.   to persuade medical personnel to speak only when necessary
   C.   to tell an interesting story about a paramedic who offended a patient
   D.   to advise medical practitioners about communicating with patients in crisis
   E.   to encourage people to join the medical field

3. What is the meaning of the phrase "speaks volumes" in the second paragraph?
   A. talks too much
   B. reads instructions
   C. communicates many things
   D. reads novels in several volumes
   E. speaks too loudly

Use the following passage for question 4.

Passage 1

Panda bears live in China's bamboo forests. They eat bamboo and are excellent tree climbers. New roads and railroads break the flow of the forest, isolating panda populations. This decreases the amount of food pandas can access during the year.

Passage 2

Polar bears live in the Arctic and are the largest land carnivores in the world. They eat seals and walruses. As the sea gets larger from melting ice, polar bears have to travel longer distances for food. Their thick white fur provides warmth and traction for their feet on the ice. They are good swimmers.

4. The authors of Passage 1 and Passage 2 would both agree with which of the following statements?
   A. Pandas should become carnivores to supplement their diet of bamboo.
   B. The destruction of habitats affects the food supply of many animals.
   C. Animals must be able to move easily in their environments.
   D. Warming weather will expand the habitats of pandas and polar bears.
   E. Eventually, panda bears and polar bears will evolve into the same species.

Use the following passage for questions 5 – 6.

The study showed that private tutoring is providing a significant advantage to those students who are able to afford it. Researchers looked at the grades of students who had received free tutoring through the school versus those whose parents had paid for private tutors. The study included 2,500 students in three high schools across four grade levels. The study found that private tutoring corresponded with a rise in grade point average (GPA) of 0.5 compared to students who used the school's free tutor service and 0.7 compared to students who used no tutoring. After reviewing the study, the board is recommending that the school restructure its free tutor service to provide a more equitable education for all students.

5. Which of the following would weaken the author's argument?
   A. if the cited study was funded by a company that provides discounted tutoring through schools
   B. if the study showed differences in standardized test scores between students at schools in different neighborhoods
   C. a statement signed by local teachers stating that they do not provide preferential treatment in the classroom or when grading
   D. a study showing that GPA does not strongly correlate with success in college
   E. poll results from students that indicate an interest in improving the school's free tutoring program

6. Which type of argument is used in the passage?
   A. emotional argument
   B. appeal to authority
   C. specific evidence
   D. rhetorical questioning

Use the following passage for questions 7 – 9.

We've been told for years that the recipe for weight loss is fewer calories in than calories out. In other words, eat less and exercise more, and your body will take care of the rest. As many of those who've tried to diet can attest, this edict doesn't always produce results. If you're one of those folks, you might have felt that you just weren't doing it right—that the failure was all your fault.

However, several new studies released this year have suggested that it might not be your fault at all. For example, a study of people who had lost a high percentage of their body weight (> 17%) in a short period of time found that they could not physically maintain their new weight. Scientists measured their resting metabolic rate and found that they'd need to consume only a few hundred calories a day to meet their metabolic needs. Basically, their bodies were in starvation mode and seemed to desperately hang on to each and every calorie. Eating even a single healthy, well-balanced meal a day would cause these subjects to start packing back on the pounds.

Other studies have shown that factors like intestinal bacteria, distribution of body fat, and hormone levels can affect the manner in which our bodies process calories. There's also the fact that it's actually quite difficult to measure the number of calories consumed during a particular meal and the number used while exercising.

7. Which of the following would be the best summary statement to conclude the passage?
   A. It turns out that conventional dieting wisdom does not capture the whole picture of how our bodies function.
   B. Still, counting calories and tracking exercise is a good idea if you want to lose weight.
   C. In conclusion, it is important to lose weight responsibly: losing too much weight at once can negatively impact the body.
   D. It is easy to see that diets don't work, so we should focus less on weight loss and more on overall health.
   E. Taking probiotics is, therefore, instrumental for long-term, successful weight loss.

8. Which type of argument is used in the passage?
   A. emotional argument
   B. appeal to authority
   C. specific evidence
   D. rhetorical questioning
   E. argument of interpretation

9. Which of the following would weaken the author's argument?
   A. discussion of a new diet pill from a pharmaceutical company that promises to help patients lose weight by changing intestinal bacteria
   B. the personal experience of a man who was able to lose a significant amount of weight by taking in fewer calories than he used
   C. a study showing that people in different geographic locations lose different amounts of weight when on the same diet
   D. a study showing that people often misreport their food intake when part of a scientific study on weight loss
   E. discussion of a new tool that can determine the amount of calories in any given meal

Questions 10 – 11 refer to the following excerpt from Address of President Roosevelt at St. Louis, Missouri, October 2, 1907:

From every standpoint it is desirable for the Nation to join in improving the greatest system of river highways within its borders, a system second only in importance to the highway afforded by the Great Lakes; the highways of the Mississippi and its great tributaries, such as the Missouri and Ohio. This river system traverses too many States to render it possible to leave merely to the States the task of fitting it for the greatest use of which it is capable. It is emphatically a national task, for this great river system is itself one of our chief national assets. Within the last few years there has been an awakening in this country to the need of both the conservation and the development of our national resources under the supervision of and by the aid of the Federal Government. This is especially true of all that concerns our running waters. On the mountains from which the springs start we are now endeavoring to preserve the forests which regulate the water supply and prevent too startling variations between droughts and freshets. Below the mountains, in the high dry regions of the western plains, we endeavor to secure the proper utilization of the waters for irrigation. This is at the sources of the streams. Farther down, where they become navigable, our aim must be to try to develop a policy which shall secure the utmost advantage from the navigable waters.

10. What is Roosevelt's central claim?
    A. The US has many important natural resources.
    B. The states have done a poor job in waterway management.
    C. Waterway management is a job for the federal government.
    D. Natural resources must be conserved as part of the national agenda.
    E. States should show more concern for national conservation efforts.

11. Roosevelt would MOST likely agree with which of the following statements?
    A. The gifts of nature belong only to those who seek them out.
    B. Local government most often knows what is best for its constituents.
    C. States should lead conservation efforts for all nature within their boundaries.
    D. Limited government is the best type as it gives greater voice to the people.
    E. Careful planning is necessary to get the most out of what nature offers.

Use the following passage for questions 12 – 13.

Across the globe, women are, on average, outliving their male counterparts. Although this gender gap has shrunk over the last decade thanks to medical improvements and lifestyle changes, women are still expected to live four and a half years longer than men. What is the reason for this trend? The answer may lie in our sex hormones.

Men are more likely to exhibit riskier behaviors than women, especially between the ages of fifteen and twenty-four, when testosterone production is at its peak. Testosterone is correlated with aggressive and reckless behaviors that contribute to high mortality rates—think road rage, alcohol consumption, drug use, and smoking.

Estrogen, on the other hand, seems to be correlated with cholesterol levels: an increase in estrogen is accompanied by a decrease in "bad" cholesterol, which may confer advantages by reducing the risk of heart attack and stroke.

Of course, lifestyle and diet are also components of this difference in life expectancy. Men are more likely to be involved in more physically dangerous jobs, such as manufacturing or construction. They may be less likely to eat as many fruits and vegetables as their female counterparts. And they may be more likely to consume more red meat, including processed meat. These types of meats have been linked to high cholesterol, hypertension, and cancer. Better nutrition and health decisions may eventually even the score in men's and women's life expectancies.

12. What inference can the reader make based on the essay?
    A. Men must work harder than women to achieve the same health outcomes.
    B. Women's life spans are increasing while men's life spans are decreasing.
    C. Both women and men have hormones that cause troubling health outcomes.
    D. Men's lifestyle choices have stayed the same while women's have improved with time.
    E. Women must use supplements if they wish to extend their average life expectancy.

13. What is the BEST reason for the author to consider deleting the last paragraph?
    A. It offers strategies for men to increase their life expectancy.
    B. It refutes the earlier point that hormones are the reason for differences in life expectancy.
    C. It introduces a counterclaim for the notion that women tend to outlive men.
    D. It makes a direct comparison between the health choices men and women are most likely to make.
    E. It makes inaccurate assumptions.

Use the following passage for questions 14 – 15.

Understanding the distribution of water in our solar system tells us a great deal about how the planets, moons, comets, and other bodies formed 4.5 billion years ago from the disk of gas and dust that surrounded our sun. The space closer to the sun was hotter and drier than the space farther from the sun, which was cold enough for water to condense. The dividing line, called the "frost line," sat around Jupiter's present-day orbit. Even today, this is the approximate distance from the sun at which the ice on most comets begins to melt and become "active." Their brilliant spray releases water ice, vapor, dust, and other chemicals which are thought to form the bedrock of most worlds of the frigid outer solar system.

14. The structure of the passage is primarily
    A. problem-solution.
    B. compare/contrast.
    C. descriptive.
    D. narrative.
    E. argumentative.

15. Based on the passage, what is necessary for water in space?
    A. dust
    B. cool temperatures
    C. warm temperatures
    D. chemicals
    E. gas

Use the following passage for questions 16 – 17.

Archaeologists have discovered the oldest known specimens of bedbugs in a cave in Oregon where humans once lived. The three different species date back to between 5,000 and 11,000 years ago. The finding gives scientists a clue as to how bedbugs became human parasites. These bedbugs, like those that plague humans today, originated as bat parasites. Scientists hypothesize that it was the co-habitation of humans and bats in the caves that encouraged the bugs to begin feeding on the humans. The three species found in the Oregon caves are actually still around today, although they continue to prefer bats; however, humans only lived seasonally in the Oregon cave system, which might explain why these insects did not fully transfer to human hosts like bedbugs elsewhere did.

16. What is the most likely reason that the author includes the last sentence of the paragraph?
    A. to concede that further bedbug research is needed
    B. to suggest that bedbugs are continually adapting
    C. to connect bedbug research to broader human migrations
    D. to explain why this bedbug species still prefers bats
    E. to reassure the audience that bedbugs no longer pose a threat to humans

17. The author's purpose is most likely to
    A. explain why bedbugs began to feed on humans.
    B. highlight the importance of a groundbreaking study.
    C. refute major beliefs people erroneously believe.
    D. describe the relationship between bats and bedbugs.
    E. educate the public on bedbug eradication

Use the following passage for questions 18 – 19.

1)) Learning to play tennis well involves getting the stroke down. 2)) A forehand stroke involves the use of only one hand and often employs topspin created by a wrist motion. 3)) Many people hit the backhand with two hands, though this has only become popular in modern times. 4)) The two-handed backhand surged in popularity after being used by phenom Chris Evert. 5)) The primary advantage to hitting the backhand stroke with two hands is increased power and spin. 6)) One other option is the backhand slice, which is sort of a downward, chopping motion with one hand that creates wicked spin and a ball that seems to drop suddenly. 7)) Each individual will have to determine the strokes that feel the most natural and which fit into his or her game the best.

18. Which sentence is least related to the overall topic of the paragraph and can be eliminated?
    A. sentence 2
    B. sentence 3
    C. sentence 4
    D. sentence 6
    E. sentence 5

19. Which word from the paragraph is used to mean "hard to hit"?
    A. chopping
    B. wicked
    C. suddenly
    D. natural
    E. topspin

Questions 20 – 22 refer to the following text excerpt from Black Beauty by Anna Sewell.

The name of the coachman was John Manly; he had a wife and one little child, and they lived in the coachman's cottage, very near the stables.

The next morning he took me into the yard and gave me a good grooming, and just as I was going into my box, with my coat soft and bright, the squire came in to look at me, and seemed pleased. "John," he said, "I meant to have tried the new horse this morning, but I have other business. You may as well take him around after breakfast; go by the common and the Highwood, and back by the watermill and the river; that will show his paces."

"I will, sir," said John. After breakfast he came and fitted me with a bridle. He was very particular in letting out and taking in the straps, to fit my head comfortably; then he brought a saddle, but it was not broad enough for my back; he saw it in a minute and went for another, which fitted nicely. He rode me first slowly, then a trot, then a canter, and when we were on the common he gave me a light touch with his whip, and we had a splendid gallop.

20. Which inference can the reader make based on the text?
    A. John Manly does not like his job.
    B. John Manly has respect for horses.
    C. John Manly is a coachman with a family.
    D. John Manly has bought a new horse.
    E. John Manley does not respect the squire.

21. Which point of view is used by the author?
    A. first-person
    B. second-person
    C. third-person objective
    D. third-person omniscient
    E. third-person limited

22. Which of the following is the best summary of the excerpt?
    A. John Manly is a coachman who lives with his wife and a child in a cottage near a set of stables. He works in the stables grooming horses for the squire.
    B. After he has breakfast, John Manly has a splendid gallop by the watermill and along the river with a new horse from the stables.
    C. The horse is new to the stables, but the squire does not have time to check his paces, so he asks John Manly to do it, but John has to have breakfast first.
    D. The coachman, John Manly, grooms the horse and fits him comfortably with a bridle and saddle. He then takes the horse for a ride to test the horse's paces for the squire.
    E. The squire is a busy man who is overwhelmed and cannot properly care for his horses.

Use the following passage for question 23.

For thirteen years, a spacecraft called *Cassini* was on an exploratory mission to Saturn. The spacecraft was designed not to return but to end its journey by diving into Saturn's atmosphere. This dramatic ending provided scientists with unprecedented information about Saturn's atmosphere and its magnetic and gravitational fields. First, however, *Cassini* passed Saturn's largest moon, Titan, where it recorded data on Titan's curious methane lakes, gathering information about potential seasons on the planet-sized moon. Then it passed through the unexplored region between Saturn itself and its famous rings. Scientists hope to learn how old the rings are and to directly examine the particles that make them up. *Cassini's* mission ended in 2017, but researchers have new questions for future exploration.

23. According to the passage, scientists want to learn more about Titan's
   A.   gravity, based on examination of its magnetic field.
   B.   rings, based on the particles that compose them.
   C.   seasons, based on changes to its lakes.
   D.   age, based on analysis of its minerals and gases.
   E.   atmosphere, based on measurements of its gravity.

Use the following passage for question 24.

Tourists flock to Yellowstone National Park each year to view the geysers that bubble and erupt throughout it. What most of these tourists do not know is that these geysers are formed by a caldera, a hot crater in the earth's crust, that was created by a series of three eruptions of an ancient supervolcano. These eruptions, which began 2.1 million years ago, spewed between 1,000 to 2,450 cubic kilometers of volcanic matter at such a rate that the volcano's magma chamber collapsed, creating the craters.

24. What is the main idea of the passage?
   A.   Yellowstone National Park is a popular tourist destination.
   B.   The geysers in Yellowstone National Park rest on a caldera in the earth's crust.
   C.   A supervolcano once sat in the area covered by Yellowstone National Park.
   D.   The earth's crust is weaker in Yellowstone National Park.
   E.   Yellowstone National Park is at risk of a volcanic eruption.

Use the following passage for questions 25 – 26.

The odds of success for any new restaurant are slim. Competition in the city is fierce, and the low margin of return means that aspiring restaurateurs must be exact and ruthless with their budgets and pricing. The fact that The Hot Dog has lasted as long as it has is a testament to its owner's skills.

25. Which of the following conclusions is well supported by the passage?
   A.   The Hot Dog offers the best casual dining in town.
   B.   The Hot Dog has a well-managed budget and prices items on its menu appropriately.
   C.   The popularity of The Hot Dog will likely fall as new restaurants open in the city.
   D.   The Hot Dog has a larger margin of return than other restaurants in the city.
   E.   The owner of The Hot Dog is optimistic about the restaurant's long-term success.

26. Which of the following is the meaning of the word *testament* as used in the sentence?
    A. story
    B. surprise
    C. artifact
    D. evidence
    E. promise

Use the following passage for question 27.

The social and political discourse of America continues to be permeated with idealism. An idealistic viewpoint asserts that the ideals of freedom, equality, justice, and human dignity are the truths that Americans must continue to aspire to. Idealists argue that truth is what should be, not necessarily what is. In general, they work to improve things and to make them as close to ideal as possible.

27. Which of the following best captures the author's purpose?
    A. to advocate for freedom, equality, justice, and human rights
    B. to explain what an idealist believes in
    C. to explain what's wrong with social and political discourse in America
    D. to persuade readers to believe in certain truths
    E. to encourage readers to question the truth

Questions 28 – 29 refer to the following passage, taken from the speech "The Man with the Muck-Rake" by Theodore Roosevelt, delivered 14 April 1906.

Over a century ago Washington laid the corner stone of the Capitol in what was then little more than a tract of wooded wilderness here beside the Potomac. We now find it necessary to provide by great additional buildings for the business of the government.

This growth in the need for the housing of the government is but a proof and example of the way in which the nation has grown and the sphere of action of the national government has grown. We now administer the affairs of a nation in which the extraordinary growth of population has been outstripped by the growth of wealth in complex interests. The material problems that face us today are not such as they were in Washington's time, but the underlying facts of human nature are the same now as they were then. Under altered external form we war with the same tendencies toward evil that were evident in Washington's time, and are helped by the same tendencies for good. It is about some of these that I wish to say a word today.

28. What is the central idea of Roosevelt's speech?
    A. The growth of the United States has resulted in a war between the conflicting interests of many groups in government.
    B. While the US government and population have grown, the United States continues to deal with the basic characteristics of human nature, both positive and negative.
    C. Many Americans have gained great wealth and are now attempting to control the government.
    D. The country has grown so fast and has acquired so much wealth that the government is struggling to deal with rising inequality between the wealthy and the poor.
    E. Congress must approve funding for additional government buildings.

29. Roosevelt mentions construction of "great additional buildings for the business of government" to emphasize
    A.   changes that have taken place in the type of government.
    B.   the complexity of democratic principles.
    C.   the power of the United States as a world leader.
    D.   the growth of the United States.
    E.   the inferiority of the original buildings in Washington, D.C.

Use the following passage for questions 30 – 31.

Skin coloration and markings have an important role to play in the world of snakes. Those intricate diamonds, stripes, and swirls help the animals hide from predators, but perhaps most importantly (for us humans, anyway), the markings can also indicate whether the snake is venomous. While it might seem counterintuitive for a venomous snake to stand out in bright red or blue, that fancy costume tells any nearby predator that approaching him would be a bad idea. If you see a flashy-looking snake in the woods, though, those markings don't necessarily mean it's venomous: some snakes have found a way to ward off predators without the actual venom. The scarlet kingsnake, for example, has very similar markings to the venomous coral snake with whom it frequently shares a habitat. However, the kingsnake is actually nonvenomous; it's merely pretending to be dangerous to eat. A predatory hawk or eagle, usually hunting from high in the sky, can't tell the difference between the two species, and so the kingsnake gets passed over and lives another day.

30. What is the primary purpose of this passage?
    A.   to explain how markings on snakes are related to whether they are venomous
    B.   to teach readers the difference between coral snakes and kingsnakes
    C.   to illustrate why snakes are dangerous
    D.   to demonstrate how animals survive in difficult environments
    E.   to disprove popular notions of the snake species

31. Which of the following is the best summary of this passage?
    A.   Humans can use coloration and markings on snakes to determine whether they're venomous.
    B.   Animals often use coloration to hide from predators.
    C.   The scarlet kingsnake and the coral snake have nearly identical markings.
    D.   Venomous snakes often have bright markings, although nonvenomous snakes can also mimic those colors.
    E.   The coral snake and the kingsnake are birds of prey, like hawks and eagles, pose a danger to both venomous and nonvenomous snake species and are especially dangerous to humans.

Use the following passage for questions 32 – 35.

Sugar is an essential fuel for the human body; however, Americans, on average, are consuming twenty *more* teaspoons of sugar daily than the American Heart Association's recommendation of six teaspoons for women and nine for men. The reason for this excess is twofold: humans may have an evolutionary hunger for sugar, and food companies are capitalizing on this human sweet tooth. As a result, millions of Americans are suffering from obesity, diabetes, and tooth decay.

When the body breaks down food, it only uses some simple sugars for immediate energy; the rest of the sugar is stored as fat that can be called upon for energy later. The issue is that millions of people are storing too much fat because they are simply eating too much sugar. In addition to its obvious sources—cake, cookies, soda—added sugar lurks in many supposedly healthy foods, such as tomato sauce, yogurt, granola, and fruit snacks. In particular, low-fat versions of some of these foods are packed with extra sugar to improve the flavor lost by reducing the fat content.

Foods that naturally contain sugar offer a healthy alternative to processed foods with added sugar. The naturally occurring sugar in fruits and vegetables is accompanied by fiber and other nutritional elements. That is why health professionals recommend that children trade in their cans of soda for a handful of grapes or a plate of sweet potatoes. These so-called smart sweets help Americans satiate their sugar fix while also giving them the appropriate fuel to enjoy a healthy life.

32. What is the main idea of the passage?
  A.   Sugar provides fuel for the human body.
  B.   Consuming too much sugar causes obesity, diabetes, and tooth decay.
  C.   Experts say that Americans eat too much sugar.
  D.   Foods such as tomato sauce, yogurt, and granola contain added sugar.
  E.   Although overconsumption of sugar should be avoided, it is riskier to not eat any sugar.

33. What is the meaning of the word *fuel* in the first sentence?
  A.   energy source
  B.   gas or gasoline
  C.   petroleum
  D.   stimulate
  E.   health risk

34. Which of the following is not listed as a detail in the passage?
  A.   The American Heart Association recommends that women consume only six teaspoons of sugar per day.
  B.   Human beings may have evolved to crave sugar.
  C.   Some sugar is stored as fat; the body can use fat for energy at a later time.
  D.   Corn syrup, an ingredient in some foods, contains a great deal of sugar.
  E.   The body only needs some simple sugars for immediate energy.

35. Which of the following statements can readers infer from the passage?
  A.   If you are a man and you consume ten teaspoons of sugar per day, you are certainly endangering your health.
  B.   If you are a woman and you consume twenty-six teaspoons of sugar per day, you are likely to be—or to become—overweight.
  C.   If you are a child and you drink one sugary soda drink per day, you are sure to have tooth decay.
  D.   Homo sapiens living in prehistoric times were unable to find enough sugar to fuel their bodies.
  E.   It is better to eat full-fat foods in order to avoid the sugars used to replace fat in low-fat foods.

Use the following passage for questions 36 – 39.

Empathy is different from mimicry or sympathy—it is neither imitating someone else's emotions nor feeling concern for their suffering. Empathy is much more complex; it is the ability to actually share and comprehend the emotions of others.

Empathy takes on two major forms: cognitive empathy and affective, or emotional, empathy. Cognitive empathy is the ability to identify and understand the emotions, mental state, or perspective of others. Affective empathy is the ability to experience an emotional response to the emotions of others—either to feel what they are feeling or to have an appropriate emotional reaction, such as feeling sad when hearing about someone's bad news. Related to affective empathy is compassionate empathy—the ability to control your own emotions while helping others deal with theirs.

Empathy is crucial for being able to respond properly in social settings. People who suffer from some psychiatric conditions, such as autism spectrum disorder, may struggle with being empathetic. Conversely, some people with very strong cognitive empathy may abuse their social understanding as a means to take advantage of others. Most people, however, choose moments and contexts in which they are likely to relate to the emotions of others.

36. What can the reader infer that the author believes about empathy?
    A. It is a primarily positive quality.
    B. It is similar to autism spectrum disorder.
    C. It is similar to mimicry or sympathy.
    D. It is a good quality is some cases and a bad quality in others.
    E. It is an emotional skill that few people possess.

37. What is the author's primary purpose in writing these paragraphs?
    A. to define empathy
    B. to persuade readers to show more empathy
    C. to advise readers about ways to appear empathetic
    D. to show that empathy is a better quality than sympathy
    E. to encourage readers to learn more about people's emotions

38. According to the passage, what is one negative use of empathy?
    A. People who actually possess little or no empathy may fake this quality.
    B. People who are empathetic may feel too much concern for others' suffering.
    C. People with affective empathy may experience an emotional response to others' emotions.
    D. People with strong empathy toward others tend to be taken advantage of.
    E. People with strong cognitive empathy may abuse this knowledge.

39. Readers can infer that _____ might be most useful to a medical professional who responds to emergencies.
    A. sympathy and mimicry
    B. cognitive empathy
    C. affective empathy
    D. compassionate empathy
    E. false empathy

Use the following passage for questions 40 – 45.

The history of vaccines dates back further than one might imagine—all the way to tenth-century China, where smallpox scabs were ground up and blown into a person's nostrils. However, what we recognize as the precursor to the modern vaccine came in 1796. English surgeon Edward Jenner built on the knowledge that people who worked with cows and had been exposed to cowpox, which has a mild effect on humans, did not catch smallpox. Jenner deliberately exposed a child to cowpox by taking some of the serum from a pustule on the hand of a milkmaid and scratching it into the child's skin. Six weeks later, he exposed the child to smallpox—and the child remained healthy.

Vaccines work by stimulating the immune system to produce antibodies against a particular disease. How does this happen? A minute amount of the disease-producing pathogen is injected into the bloodstream (although some vaccines can be taken orally or even as a nasal spray). The pathogen is either present in such a small amount that it will not cause illness or the pathogen is "dead." Either way, you cannot get sick, but your immune system will ramp up to repel the invaders. Your immune system hangs on to the antibodies it creates; if you are exposed to the pathogen in the future, your body is ready to fight it off.

Vaccines have been crucial components in the long history of public health efforts in the United States and have helped eradicate or almost eradicate previously widespread diseases such as whooping cough, polio, rubella, tetanus, tuberculosis, smallpox, diphtheria, and measles. The creation of the National Vaccine Agency in 1813 encouraged many states to adopt mandatory immunizations for schoolchildren for the first time. Today, every state requires some immunizations for children entering public schools, though all allow medical exemptions and most allow exemptions on religious or philosophical grounds.

40. What does the first paragraph mainly concern?
    A. smallpox vaccines in tenth-century China
    B. Jenner's smallpox vaccine in 1796
    C. a cure for cowpox in the late 1700s
    D. wiping out widespread diseases in the United States
    E. the relationship between cowpox and farming

41. What is the author's primary purpose in writing this essay?
    A. to warn parents about possible side effects of vaccines
    B. to persuade parents to have their children vaccinated
    C. to advise people about different treatments for infectious diseases
    D. to inform readers about the history of vaccines, including how they work
    E. to encourage readers to consider alternative medicine

42. Which of the following statements can be considered a statement of fact according to the content offered in the paragraphs above?
    A. Chinese doctors were the first to successfully cure smallpox.
    B. A vaccine works with the body's immune system to prevent someone from getting a disease.
    C. Thanks to Edward Jenner, diseases such as whooping cough and polio no longer exist.
    D. Thanks to worldwide vaccination programs, most infectious diseases will soon be eradicated.
    E. Eastern medicines laid the groundwork for today's vaccines.

43. According to the passage, what is true about state laws on vaccinating schoolchildren?
    A. There are no exceptions to these requirements.
    B. The only exceptions to these laws are for medical reasons.
    C. Everyone should obey these laws because diseases are infectious.
    D. Most states have religious and philosophical exemptions to these laws.
    E. State laws concerning vaccinations for schoolchildren are reevaluated every election cycle.

44. Readers can infer that neither _____ nor the common cold have been eradicated or close to eradicated in the United States.
    A. all flu viruses
    B. the measles
    C. tetanus
    D. tuberculosis
    E. meningitis

45. What is the meaning of the word *immunizations* in the last paragraph?
    A. immune systems
    B. pathogens
    C. pustules
    D. checkups
    E. vaccinations

Use the following passage for questions 46 – 50.

If you frequent your local health food store, you will likely come across a popular international spice: turmeric. Turmeric comes from the bulbous root of a plant known as *Curcuma longa*. It is related to ginger, but the fleshy inside of the root is a deep yellow. Once the root is boiled, dried, and ground, it creates a bitter yellow powdered spice that gives Indian curry its distinctive color. Turmeric has been used medicinally—as well as in cooking, as a dye, and in religious rituals—in India and Southeast Asia for millennia. Its anti-inflammatory properties have gained the adoration of Western health and wellness gurus in recent years.

Today, many Americans are touting turmeric as a holistic medicinal replacement for anti-inflammatory drugs. Small-scale studies have shown that curcumin, a key compound found in turmeric, can help with both skin inflammation and joint inflammation. Companies are adding turmeric to topical creams for skin care, and patients with rheumatoid arthritis are taking their daily dose of turmeric pills to help decrease pain and stiffness in their joints. Larger-scale clinical studies have not provided conclusive evidence for these benefits.

Regardless of its true health benefits, expect to see turmeric continue to impact the health food and holistic medicine industries in the near future. It is hard to walk through any upscale health food store without seeing the buzzword *turmeric* plastered on trendy juices and vegan powder canisters.

46. Readers can infer from the passage that the author _____
    A. believes in turmeric's anti-inflammatory health properties.
    B. is not sure that turmeric is an effective anti-inflammatory aid.
    C. uses turmeric at home to add spice to Indian cuisine.
    D. has used turmeric to dye cloth a deep yellow.
    E. suggests that people should grow turmeric at home, if possible.

47. What is the author's primary purpose in writing this essay?
    A. to persuade readers with arthritis to buy turmeric
    B. to criticize health food businesses for selling turmeric
    C. to explain what turmeric is and why it has become popular
    D. to warn consumers not to be gullible enough to buy turmeric
    E. to persuade consumers to vary the spices they use when cooking

48. Which sentence best summarizes the passage's main idea?
    A. "Turmeric comes from the bulbous root of a plant known as *Curcuma longa*."
    B. "Once the root is boiled, dried, and ground, it creates a bitter yellow powdered spice that gives Indian curry its distinctive color."
    C. "Small-scale studies have shown that curcumin, a key compound found in turmeric, can help with both skin inflammation and joint inflammation."
    D. "Regardless of its true health benefits, expect to see turmeric continue to impact the health food and holistic medicine industries in the near future."
    E. "It is related to ginger, but the fleshy inside of the root is a deep yellow."

49. According to the passage, when did people first begin to use turmeric medicinally?
    A. hundreds of years ago
    B. in the mid-1900s
    C. in the early 2000s
    D. a few years ago
    E. since prehistoric times

50. According to the passage, which types of studies have shown that turmeric is an effective medicine?
    A. studies run by wellness gurus
    B. small-scale studies
    C. larger-scale clinical studies
    D. studies run by the health food and holistic medicine industries
    E. federally funded studies

Writing

Read the prompt, and then write a short essay defending your opinion.

Topic 1

On this essay, you must effectively express and develop your ideas in writing. Read a short passage; an assignment question follows about an important issue. Develop your own point of view on the issue in the essay, and be sure to support your argument with examples and reasoning. Your personal perspective on the issue will not influence your score.

It is said that a crowd, proportionately to its size, magnifies all that in its units pertains to the emotions, and diminishes all that in them pertains to thought. The group's passion for Zuleika was so intense precisely because of its size. This rule might apply to large groups of people gathered together, or even to whole nations of individuals with shared interests.

Adapted from Max Beerbohm, Zuleika Dobson

> Is it possible for a large group of people to remain rational and thoughtful when confronted with an emotional situation?

Topic 2

Read the quotes below and write an essay using the prompt which follows. In your essay, develop your own point of view, and be sure to support your argument with examples and reasoning. Your personal perspective on the issue will not influence your score.

O judgment! Thou art fled to brutish beasts, and men have lost their reason.

– William Shakespeare, *Julius Caesar*

Don't judge a book by its cover.

– George Eliot, *The Mill on the Floss*

> Can we be too quick to judge the actions of another person?

Math

1. Some of a hotel's 400 rooms have ocean views, and the rest of the rooms do not. If the probability of getting a room with an ocean view is 35%, how many rooms do NOT have an ocean view?
    A.   65
    B.   140
    C.   200
    D.   260
    E.   300

2. Which of the following is listed in order from least to greatest? (Select all that apply.)
    A. $-0.95, 0, \frac{1}{5}, 0.35, \frac{3}{4}$

    B. $-1, -\frac{1}{10}, -0.11, \frac{5}{6}, 0.75$

    C. $-\frac{3}{4}, -0.2, 0, \frac{2}{5}, 0.55$

    D. $-1.1, -\frac{4}{5}, -0.13, 0.7, \frac{9}{11}$

    E. $-0.0001, -\frac{1}{12}, 0, \frac{2}{3}, \frac{4}{5}$

3. What is the value of 15.32×4.76?
    A.   6.02432
    B.   60.2432
    C.   72.9232
    D.   602.432
    E.   729.232

4. Aprille has $50 to buy the items on her shopping list. Assuming there is no sales tax, about how much change will Aprille receive after buying all of the items on her list?

APRILLE'S LIST	
Item	Price
hammer	$13.24
screwdriver	$11.99
nails	$4.27
wrench	$5.60

    A. $12
    B. $13
    C. $14
    D. $15
    E. $16

5. Which expression is equivalent to dividing 400 by 16?
- A. $2(200 - 8))$
- B. $(400 \div 4) \div 12$
- C. $(216 \div 8) + (184 \div 8))$
- D. $(216 \div 16) + (184 \div 16)$
- E. $(400 \div 4) \div 16$

6. Solve the following inequality for x: $2(-3x - 2) < 2$
- A. $x > -2$
- B. $x < -\frac{2}{3}$
- C. $x < -1$
- D. $x > -1$
- E. $x > 1$

7. Students board a bus at 7:45 a.m. and arrive at school at 8:20 a.m. How long are the students on the bus?
- A. 30 minutes
- B. 35 minutes
- C. 45 minutes
- D. 50 minutes
- E. 65 minutes

8. Convert 8 pounds, 8 ounces to kilograms to the nearest tenth of a kilogram.
- A. 3.9 kilograms
- B. 4.1 kilograms
- C. 17.6 kilograms
- D. 18.7 kilograms
- E. 19.36 kilograms

9. Lynn has 4 test scores in science class. Each test is worth 100 points, and Lynn has an 85% average. If Lynn scored 100% on each of the first 3 tests, what did she score on her 4th test?
- A. 40%
- B. 55%
- C. 60%
- D. 85%
- E. 100%

10. In a theater, there are 4,500 lower-level seats and 2,000 upper-level seats. What is the ratio of lower-level seats to total seats?

    A. $\frac{4}{9}$

    B. $\frac{4}{13}$

    C. $\frac{9}{13}$

    D. $\frac{9}{4}$

    E. $\frac{13}{9}$

11. The graph below shows rainfall in inches per month.

Which month had the HIGHEST total rainfall in 2002?

    A. June
    B. July
    C. August
    D. September
    E. October

12. In a game of musical chairs, there are 9 people playing and 7 available seats. Those who do not get a seat by the time the music ends are eliminated. What is the probability a person is not eliminated?

    A. 11%
    B. 22%
    C. 50%
    D. 78%
    E. 89%

13. Convert 3.28 to a fraction.

   A. $3\frac{1}{50}$

   B. $3\frac{1}{25}$

   C. $3\frac{7}{50}$

   D. $3\frac{4}{25}$

   E. $3\frac{7}{25}$

14. Convert 55 meters to feet (round to the nearest tenth of a foot).

   A.   16.8 feet
   B.   21.7 feet
   C.   139.7 feet
   D.   165.0 feet
   E.   180.4 feet

15. The cost of 2.4 yards of lumber is $24.96. What is the cost per yard?

   A. $5.99
   B. $10.40
   C. $22.46
   D. $27.36
   E. $59.90

16. Classify the number $\frac{13}{14}$.

   A.   irrational
   B.   imaginary
   C.   rational
   D.   integer
   E.   whole

17. What is the perimeter of the regular polygon?

   A.   4 in.
   B.   8 in.
   C.   10 in.
   D.   32 in.
   E.   14 in.

18. $6 \times 0 \times 5 =$
    A.   30
    B.   11
    C.   25
    D.   0
    E.   1

19. *W*, *X*, *Y*, and *Z* lie on a circle with center *A*. If the diameter of the circle is 75, what is the sum of *AW*, *AX*, *AY*, and *AZ*?
    A.   75
    B.   300
    C.   150
    D.   106.5
    E.   92

20. Examine the figure below and choose the best answer.

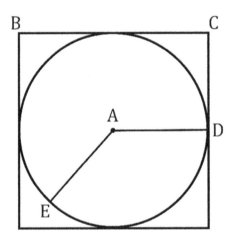

    A.   AD is equal to BC
    B.   CD is equal to half of AE
    C.   AE is greater than AD
    D.   BC is equal to AD plus AE
    E.   CD is less than AE

21. A vending machine contains 12 types of snacks. Some snacks are salty, and some snacks are sweet. The ratio of sweet snacks to salty snacks is 1:3. How many types of sweet snacks are in the vending machine?
    A.   1
    B.   3
    C.   4
    D.   12
    E.   9

22. A grocery store sold 30% of its pears and had 455 pears remaining. How many pears did the grocery store start with?
    A. 602
    B. 650
    C. 692
    D. 755
    E. 625

23. Dora commutes to work every day. During one week, her commute times were 29.15 minutes, 30.75 minutes, 28.59 minutes, 27.20 minutes, and 35.62 minutes. If the times are rounded to the nearest minute, what is the BEST estimate of the total time (in minutes) that Dora spent on her commute during this week?
    A. 151
    B. 152
    C. 150
    D. 153
    E. 148

24. Which of the following sets of shapes are all similar to each other? (Select all that apply.)
    A. right triangles
    B. spheres
    C. isosceles triangles
    D. squares
    E. cubes

25. What is the percent increase in an employee's salary if it is raised from $57,000 to $60,000?
    A. 0.3%
    B. 0.4%
    C. 3%
    D. 4%
    E. 5%

26. Using the information in the table, which equation demonstrates the linear relationship between x and y?

x	y
3	3
7	15
10	24

    A. $y = 6x - 6$
    B. $y = 5x - 6$
    C. $y = 4x - 6$
    D. $y = 3x - 6$
    E. $y = 2x - 6$

27. Which of the following is CLOSEST in value to 129,113 + 34,602?
    A. 162,000
    B. 163,000
    C. 164,000
    D. 165,000
    E. 166,000

28. Which number should fill in the blank in the series?

$$2^3, 2^2, 2^1, \underline{\quad}, 2^{-1}, 2^{-2}$$

    A. 2
    B. 1
    C. 0
    D. -1
    E. -2

29. Kim and Chris are writing a book together. Kim wrote twice as many pages as Chris, and together they wrote 240 pages. How many pages did Chris write?
    A. 80
    B. 100
    C. 120
    D. 160
    E. 240

30. Which statement about the following set is true?

$$\{60, 5, 18, 20, 37, 37, 11, 90, 72\}$$

    A. The median and the mean are equal.
    B. The mean is less than the mode.
    C. The mode is greater than the median.
    D. The median is less than the mean.
    E. The mode and the mean are equal.

31. Which of the following is listed in order from greatest to least?
    A. $\frac{1}{2}, \frac{1}{3}, \frac{1}{7}, -\frac{1}{5}, -\frac{1}{6}, -\frac{1}{4}$
    B. $\frac{1}{2}, \frac{1}{3}, \frac{1}{7}, -\frac{1}{6}, -\frac{1}{5}, -\frac{1}{4}$
    C. $\frac{1}{2}, \frac{1}{7}, \frac{1}{3}, -\frac{1}{4}, -\frac{1}{5}, -\frac{1}{6}$
    D. $\frac{1}{2}, \frac{1}{3}, \frac{1}{7}, -\frac{1}{6}, -\frac{1}{4}, -\frac{1}{5}$
    E. $\frac{1}{2}, \frac{1}{3}, \frac{1}{7}, -\frac{1}{4}, -\frac{1}{5}, -\frac{1}{6}$

32. 40% of what number is equal to 17?
    A. 2.35
    B. 6.8
    C. 42.5
    D. 235
    E. 680

33. To which of the following number sets does 3 NOT belong?
    A.   irrational
    B.   rational
    C.   whole
    D.   integer
    E.   natural

34. If $x = 5$, what is the value of the algebraic expression $2x - x$?
    A.   4
    B.   2
    C.   5
    D.   10
    E.   8

35. If $x + y$ is an odd number, which of the following MUST be true?
    A.   Both x and y must be odd numbers.
    B.   Neither x nor y can equal 0.
    C.   Either x or y is odd, while the other is even.
    D.   The product of x and y is odd.
    E. x must be larger than y.

36. Solve: $(3^2 \div 1^3) - (4 - 8^2) + 24$
    A.   −35
    B.   −4
    C.   9
    D.   28
    E.   85

37. In the decimal number 275.913, which digit is in the tenths place?
    A.   1
    B.   3
    C.   5
    D.   7
    E.   9

38. What is the value of $14.25 + 6.38 + 12.54$?
    A.   32.07
    B.   32.17
    C.   32.97
    D.   33.07
    E.   33.17

39. A food label says that the box holds 2.5 servings. How many boxes would be needed to provide 10 servings?
    A.   4 boxes
    B.   25 boxes
    C.   10 boxes
    D.   6 boxes
    E.   8 boxes

40. A second-grade teacher has completed a lesson on categorizing types of two-dimensional shapes. She draws the figure below on the board and asks her students to give a possible name for the shape.

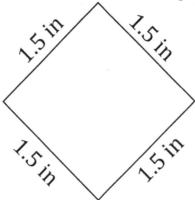

Ari says it is a rectangle, Edmundo says it is a square, Donny says it is a quadrilateral, and Gene says it is a pentagon. Which student(s) correctly named the figure?

    A.   all four students
    B.   Edmundo only
    C.   Edmundo, Donny, and Gene
    D.   Ari and Gene
    E.   Ari, Edmundo, and Donny

41. What is the square root of 169?
    A.   13
    B.   84.5
    C.   16
    D.   82
    E.   12

42. What is the probability of selecting either a king of spades or a king of clubs from a deck of 52 cards?
    A. $\frac{1}{104}$

    B. $\frac{1}{52}$

    C. $\frac{1}{26}$

    D. $\frac{3}{52}$

    E. $\frac{1}{2}$

43. Which number is equal to $(5^2 + 1))^2 + 3^3$?
    A.   703
    B.   694
    C.   30
    D.   53
    E.   402

44. Which conclusion can be drawn from the graph?

End-of-Year Grade Report

A.   More than twice as many students earned an A in science than earned an F in science.
B.   The majority of the students earned a C in math.
C.   The number of students who earned a B in reading is equal to the number of students who earned a B in math.
D.   Next year's students will not need intensive science instruction.
E.   More students earned a C in science than earned a D in science.

45. Michael is making cupcakes. He plans to give $\frac{1}{2}$ of the cupcakes to a friend and $\frac{1}{3}$ of the cupcakes to his coworkers. If he makes 48 cupcakes, how many will he have left over?
   A.   8
   B.   10
   C.   12
   D.   16
   E.   24

46. Which number has the LEAST value?
   A.   0.305
   B.   0.035
   C.   0.35
   D.   0.3
   E.   0.350

47. If a person reads 40 pages in 45 minutes, approximately how many minutes will it take her to read 265 pages?
   A.   202
   B.   236
   C.   265
   D.   298
   E.   300

48. A fruit stand sells apples, bananas, and oranges at a ratio of 3:2:1. If the fruit stand sells 20 bananas, how many TOTAL pieces of fruit does the fruit stand sell?
    A. 10
    B. 30
    C. 40
    D. 50
    E. 60

49. What is the median of the following set?
$$\{24, 27, 18, 19\}$$

    A. 19
    B. 21.5
    C. 24
    D. 25.5
    E. 27

50. Which number is 6 less than the product of 9 and 4?
    A. 9
    B. 27
    C. 5
    D. 30
    E. 12

Answer Key #2

Reading

1. C: "Medical practitioners must learn to be sensitive with people who are in crisis" is an adequate summary of the passage overall; the other options only discuss other, more specific details from the passage.

2. D: The primary purpose of the essay is to advise; its focus is how to communicate with patients in crisis. It is not persuasive or cautionary, and it does not tell a story.

3. C: In the second paragraph, the author writes, "Your body language speaks volumes." The writer then details how body language can convey messages in many ways (with "posture, hand motions, and gestures").

4. B: Both passages indicate that habitats are diminishing, impacting the animals' access to food.

5. A: A company that profits from private tutoring might introduce bias into a study on the effects of private tutoring in schools.

6. C: The author cites data from a study to support the argument.

7. A: The bulk of the passage is dedicated to showing that the conventional wisdom about "fewer calories in than calories out" is not true for many people and that weight loss is more complicated than previously believed.

8. C: The author cites several scientific studies to support the argument.

9. D: People misreporting the amount of food they eat would introduce error into studies on weight loss and might make the studies cited by the author unreliable.

10. C: Roosevelt is discussing management of large national rivers, which he believes is best handled by the federal government because these waterways are "chief national assets."

11. E: The speech is about the need for planning and policy to exploit the nation's rivers to their greatest capacity, so Roosevelt is likely to agree careful planning is necessary to get the most out of what nature offers.

12. A: The passage suggests that women have a hormonal advantage but that "better nutrition and health decisions" by men may "eventually even the score." This suggests that men may have to work harder (diet and exercise) to achieve the same longevity as women.

13. B: The last paragraph refutes the notion that hormones are responsible for women's longer life spans, which is the focus/thesis of the essay per the first paragraph. Instead, the last paragraph suggests that other factors not related to hormones, such as "lifestyle and diet," may be closely related to differences in life expectancies.

14. C: The author describes the presence of water in our solar system and where it is located.

15. B: The passage states that "The space closer to the sun was hotter and drier than the space farther from the sun, which was cold enough for water to condense." This implies that cool temperatures are needed for water.

16. D: The last sentence further explains the information presented previously about how bedbugs still prefer bats, likely because they had to feed on both humans and bats since humans were not ever-present in the cave system.

17. A: The paragraph focuses on "how bedbugs became human parasites" and uses a scientific study as evidence for this explanation.

18. C: Sentence 4 contains only background on the history of a tennis stroke, while the rest of the paragraph discusses what these strokes are and how to hit them.

19. B: In the paragraph, the word *wicked* refers to the spin on the ball being hard for the opponent to hit.

20. B: The way that John Manly takes care to make the horse comfortable before riding leads the reader to infer that he has respect for horses.

21. A: First-person point of view is written from the direct experience of one character—in this case, the horse—as indicated by the pronouns *I* and *my*.

22. D: This is the best summary because it provides a brief explanation of the excerpt's main idea and key details. It only includes the most necessary information a reader needs to comprehend the story section.

23. C: The author writes, "… it recorded data on Titan's curious methane lakes, providing information about potential seasons on the planet-sized moon."

24. B: The passage describes the origin of Yellowstone's geysers.

25. B: The passage states that restaurateurs must be "exact and ruthless with their budgets and pricing." The success of The Hot Dog implies that its owners have done that.

26. D: The word *evidence* best describes the idea that The Hot Dog's longevity is proof of its owners' skills.

27. B: The purpose of the passage is to explain what an idealist believes in. The author does not offer any opinions or try to persuade readers about the importance of certain values.

28. B: Roosevelt states his purpose when he says, "… we war with the same tendencies toward evil that were evident in Washington's time, and are helped by the same tendencies for good. It is about some of these that I wish to say a word today."

29. D: According to the text, additional government buildings have been necessary to accommodate the growth in government activity that has accompanied the corresponding growth of the country.

30. A: The passage indicates that snakes' "intricate diamonds, stripes, and swirls help the animals hide from predators, but perhaps most importantly (for us humans, anyway), the markings can also indicate whether the snake is venomous."

31. D: This summary best captures the main ideas of each paragraph.

32. C: In the second sentence, the author writes, "Americans... are consuming twenty *more* teaspoons of sugar daily than the American Heart Association's recommendation of six teaspoons for women and nine for men."

33. A: In the first sentence, the author writes, "Sugar is an essential fuel for the human body." Readers can infer from context that the author is using the word *fuel* to mean "energy source."

34. D: This detail about corn syrup is not found in the passage; however, the author does mention that some processed foods contain added sugar.

35. B: In the second sentence, the author writes that the American Heart Association recommends only six teaspoons of sugar per day for women, so twenty-six is probably far too much sugar per day unless the woman in question exercises constantly throughout the day.

36. A: In the last paragraph, the author states, "Empathy is crucial for being able to respond properly in social settings." The reader can infer from this information that empathy is a positive quality that people need in order to treat others in a socially acceptable manner.

37. A: The primary purpose of the essay is to inform; its focus is on the definition of empathy. It is not persuasive or advisory. The author does not set out to show that one quality is better than another.

38. E: In the last paragraph, the author writes, "Some people with very strong cognitive empathy may abuse their social understanding as a means to take advantage of others." Earlier the author defines "cognitive empathy" as "the ability to identify and understand the emotions, mental state, or perspective of others."

39. D: In the second paragraph, the author defines compassionate empathy as "the ability to control your own emotions while helping others deal with theirs." Readers can infer that this kind of empathy would be useful to medical professionals who have to remain calm in emergencies (when patients and bystanders are often upset).

40. B: The first paragraph tells how, in 1796, surgeon Edward Jenner invented a precursor to the modern smallpox vaccine.

41. D: The primary purpose of the essay is to inform; its focus is the history of vaccines. It is not persuasive or cautionary, and it does not give advice.

42. B: In the second paragraph, the author writes, "Vaccines work by stimulating the immune system to produce antibodies against a particular disease... Your immune system hangs on to the antibodies it creates; if you are exposed to the pathogen in the future, your body is ready to fight it off."

43. D: In the last sentence, the author writes, "Today, every state requires some immunizations for children entering public schools, though all allow medical exemptions and most allow exemptions on religious or philosophical grounds." There are no sentences supporting the other claims.

44. A: In the last paragraph, the author writes, "Vaccines... have helped eradicate or almost eradicate previously widespread diseases such as whooping cough, polio, rubella, tetanus, tuberculosis, smallpox, diphtheria, and measles." Readers can infer from this and from their own experiences that, despite flu shots, many people in the United States still get sick with the flu.

45. E: Injecting patients with vaccines (vaccinating them) immunizes them, which means that it makes the patients immune to diseases. Here, the nouns *vaccination* and *immunization* are synonyms.

Answer Key #2

46. B: The second paragraph ends with this statement: "Larger-scale clinical studies have not provided conclusive evidence for these benefits." By "these benefits," the author is referring to claims that turmeric can heal inflammation. The last paragraph begins with "Regardless of its true health benefits..." The author goes on to summarize how popular turmeric has become. The reader can infer that the author does not think there is proof for turmeric's effectiveness as an anti-inflammatory health aid.

47. C: The primary purpose of the essay is to explain; its focus is on the history of turmeric, its uses, and current popularity. The essay is not persuasive or cautionary. The author's tone is mildly critical or ironic, but the author does not seem worried that consumers will be duped by all the "buzz" about turmeric.

48. D: The passage is mainly about turmeric's current popularity among people who believe in the spice's health benefits. The other sentences provide details that support the main idea.

49. A: In the first paragraph, the author writes, "Turmeric has been used medicinally—as well as in cooking, as a dye, and in religious rituals—in India and Southeast Asia for millennia." A millennium is one hundred years, and the plural *millennia* refers to at least two hundred years.

50. B: In the second paragraph, the author writes, "Small-scale studies have shown that curcumin, a key compound found in turmeric, can help with both skin inflammation and joint inflammation."

Writing

Prompt 1

History provides countless examples of crowds that have become unruly, dangerous, even deadly. However, a commanding leader can make a difference. When a charismatic leader harnesses the emotions of the crowd, he or she can stir it up or calm it down with thoughtful and evocative words and actions. During the Great Depression, US President Franklin D. Roosevelt's speeches and "Fireside Chats" calmed Americans fearful of losing their savings and quelled financial panic. However, powerful speakers have the power to trigger violence. In the 1930s, Adolf Hitler's nationalist speeches in Germany inspired anti-Semitism, racism, and violent acts like Kristallnacht. A large crowd can remain calm in an emotional situation, but only with the right leadership.

Consumer panic makes an economic crisis into a catastrophe when people withdraw their funds from banks all at once, and social unrest can soon follow. FDR's public speeches and radio addresses, known as "Fireside Chats," were intended to calm the public while allowing bank reform and economic recovery to occur. Famously, in describing emergency measures to close the banks, he explained economic policy in plain language, reassuring Americans that their money would still be available when banks reopened. He also stayed positive and optimistic, using euphemisms like "bank holiday" and "inconvenience." His word choice and demeanor encouraged people to stay calm and cooperate with financial reforms. In fact, in his inaugural address, he proclaimed that there was "nothing to fear but fear itself," inspiring faith rather than panic in a time of national crisis when social unrest was feared.

On the other hand, Adolf Hitler rose to power in Germany on a platform of nationalism and discrimination. At the time, much like the United States, Germany was suffering from an economic depression and struggling to rebuild following the First World War. Unlike FDR, Hitler used negative language and scapegoated minority groups, especially Jewish people. He encouraged violence among his followers such as book-burnings, property damage, and deadly acts against Jewish people and other minority groups. As the Nazis became more powerful, Jewish people were subject to discriminatory laws and oppressive treatment. Jewish businesses were attacked and looted on Kristallnacht. Hitler's harsh rhetoric had contributed to a social and political environment where this abuse was acceptable, and it led to the Holocaust.

Overall, crowds are driven by emotion, and even people who remain rational within them cannot take control. Some people helped the Jews and other persecuted people in Nazi Germany, but they did so in secret, no match for the power of Hitler and Nazi ideology over the nation. Yet, as shown by FDR's leadership during the Great Depression, it is possible for a huge group—an entire nation—to stave off irrational, panicky behavior even with something as important as money. A crowd, despite its essential emotional nature, can be rendered rational and calm by the right leader.

Answer Explanation

This essay demonstrates outstanding critical thinking by developing a nuanced argument even while answering the question: "A large crowd can remain calm in an emotional situation, but only with the right leadership." The writer uses two strong examples— FDR's speeches and "Fireside Chats" and Hitler's negative language and scapegoating—contrasting them and developing the examples with specific details. Organization is clear; the thesis is presented in the introduction, a paragraph is devoted to each example, and the conclusion compares the two, highlighting FDR's calming abilities and supporting the argument. The writer uses varied sentence structure, strong vocabulary, and transition words. There are few, if any, mechanical errors.

Prompt 2

All people make mistakes, and it is easy to judge them from the outside. However, sometimes people behave in harmful ways as a result of unseen hardships. People should refrain from judgment until they have the full story. Still, an unusual challenge does not absolve someone from all responsibilities. Even those at a disadvantage are accountable for their responsibilities, but they may be forgiven for certain harms as long as they take steps to rectify them.

For instance, my parents do not get along with their neighbor because he has a messy yard, which brings down their property value. He also has a dog which he lets wander on the streets. My parents' dog, on the other hand, must stay in the house and is only allowed to run freely behind the fence in the yard or at a dog park. However, everyone in the area has approximately the same income. Furthermore, the neighbor is seemingly in good physical health and works normal hours. There seems to be no reason that he cannot spend a little time each week on yard work and keep his dogs in his yard like everyone else; however, he does have one unique characteristic: allergies.

The neighbor's health situation presents a dilemma. While he is responsible for cleaning his yard, he struggles with yardwork because his allergies prevent him from spending too much time among shrubs, bushes, and trees. In addition, it is hard for him to keep his dog in his house for long periods of time, as pet dander makes his allergies worse, but the more time the dog spends in the yard, the messier the yard gets. And on top of all that, he lives alone, with no one to help with chores. Meanwhile, both of my parents enjoy outdoor activity, have no allergies, and can tackle yardwork together quite easily. They are able to keep their dog inside without any health concerns and can take turns walking him. Taking these differences into account, it becomes clearer why the neighbor's yard is in disarray and why his dog is often out. These issues may be less about his character than his circumstances.

Still, the neighbor has a responsibility to those around him. First, he should not have a dog if he cannot properly care for it or keep it in his home. Not only is a dog roaming the streets a nuisance to other neighbors, but it is unsafe for the dog, which could be hit by a car or injured in some other way. Next, he should find a way to properly care for his yard. Perhaps he could pursue medical treatment for his allergies, hire workers to assist periodically, or even ask a friend, family member, or neighbor for assistance if his budget is tight. Even if he is struggling to care for his yard, as a homeowner he is responsible for it.

In this case, the neighbor could be forgiven if he took steps to fix the situation, because he is clearly at a disadvantage when it comes to yardwork and pet care due to his allergies, which are not his fault. However, if he does not take responsibility and make amends, his disadvantages do not matter, and he should not be forgiven. At that point, he could be judged as a poor neighbor or as a person of poor character because he has chosen to remain a nuisance in the neighborhood despite other options.

Answer Explanation

This essay demonstrates outstanding critical thinking, developing a nuanced argument even while answering the question. ("Even those at a disadvantage are accountable for their responsibilities, but they may be forgiven for certain harms as long as they take steps to rectify them.") The writer supports the argument with one anecdotal example, but the level of detail in the scenario is sufficient to illustrate the author's argument that some disadvantages may be hidden; therefore, one should not be quick to judge. ("There seems to be no reason that he cannot spend a little time each week on yard work; however, he does have one unique characteristic: allergies.") The author offers possible solutions to the harms the neighbor brings on the neighborhood, which would allow him to be forgiven ("he could pursue medical treatment... hire workers to assist... or even ask a friend, family member, or neighbor for assistance" in cleaning the yard). The writing and organization is clear and coherent; the thesis is presented in the introduction, and the anecdotal scenario is fully developed. The writer uses varied sentence structure, strong vocabulary, and transition words. There are few, if any, mechanical errors.

Math

1. D: The probability of getting a room without an ocean view is equal to 1 minus the probability of getting a room with an ocean view.

2. A, D: Write each value in decimal form and compare:

A. $-0.95 < 0 < 0.2 < 0.35 < 0.75$

B. $-1 < -0.1 < -0.11 < 0.8\overline{3} < 0.75$

C. $-0.75 < -0.2 < 0 < 0.6\overline{6} < 0.55$

D. $-1.1 < -0.8 < -0.13 < 0.7 < 0.8\overline{1}$

E. $-0.0001 < -0.8\overline{3} < 0 < 0.6\overline{6} < 0.8$

3. C: Multiply the values without the decimal points, and then move the decimal so that the final answer has 4 values to the right of the decimal.

$$1532 \times 476 = 729{,}232 \rightarrow \mathbf{72.9232}$$

4. D: To estimate the amount of the change, round the price of each item to the nearest dollar amount and subtract from the total.

$$\$50 - (\$13 + \$12 + \$4 + \$6)$$
$$= \$50 - \$35 = \textbf{\$15}$$

5. D: Solve inside the parenthesis first, and then add as follows: $(216 \div 16) + (184 \div 16) = 13.5 + 11.5 = 25$.

6. D: Isolate the variable on the left side of the inequality. Reverse the direction of the inequality when dividing by a negative number.

$$2(-3x - 2) < 2$$
$$-6x - 4 < 2$$
$$-6x < 6$$
$$\boldsymbol{x > -1}$$

7. B: There are 15 minutes between 7:45 a.m. and 8:00 a.m. and 20 minutes between 8:00 a.m. and 8:20 a.m.

$$15 \text{ minutes} + 20 \text{ minutes} = \textbf{35 minutes}$$

8. A: Multiply by the conversion factor to get from pounds to kilograms.

$$8 \text{ pounds}, 8 \text{ ounces} = 8.5 \text{ pounds}$$
$$8.5 \text{ lb} \left(\frac{1 \text{ kg}}{2.2 \text{ lb}}\right) = \textbf{3.9 kg}$$

9. A: To calculate the average, add all of the scores and divide by the total number of scores. Use the variable *x* in place of the missing score.

10. C:

$$\text{total seats} = 4{,}500 + 2{,}000$$
$$\frac{\text{lower seats}}{\text{all seats}} = \frac{4{,}500}{6{,}500} = \frac{\textbf{9}}{\textbf{13}}$$

11. C: The key shows that the light-gray top bar represents 2002. The longest bar for 2002 is in **August**, which corresponds to approximately 4.3 inches of rain.

12. D: There are 7 seats and 9 people playing. There is a 7 out of 9 chance or 78% chance a person is not eliminated.

13. E: Place the decimal over 100 and simplify.

$$\frac{28}{100} = \frac{7}{25}$$
$$3.28 = 3\frac{7}{25}$$

14. E: Multiply by the conversion factor to get from meters to feet.

$$55 \, m \left(\frac{3.28 \, ft}{1 \, m}\right) = \textbf{180.4 feet}$$

15. B: $24.96 \div 2.4 = \$10.40$

16. C: The number $\frac{13}{14}$ is rational because it can be written as a fraction but not as a whole number (without the fraction). It is not imaginary because it does not have an i component.

17. C: Add the length of each side to find the perimeter: $2 \text{ in.} + 2 \text{ in.} + 2 \text{ in.} + 2 \text{ in.} + 2 \text{ in.} = 10 \text{ in.}$

18. D: Anything multiplied by zero results in zero as the answer. In this case, 0 is being multiplied by 5 and 6, so the answer is still 0.

19. C: All of the points lie on the circle, so each line segment is a radius. The sum of the 4 lines will be 4 times the radius:

$$r = \frac{75}{2} = 37.5$$

$$4r = \mathbf{150}$$

20. D: AD and AE are both radii of circle A, so AD plus AE is equal to the diameter of the circle. BC is also equal to the diameter of the circle.

21. B: Total snacks $= 12$.

The numbers on both sides of the ratio must equal 12. If both sides of the ratio are multiplied by 3, the ratio of salty to sweet would be $3:9$.

$$\mathbf{3 \text{ sweet snacks}} + 9 \text{ salty snacks} = 12 \text{ total snacks}$$

22. B: Set up an equation. If p is the original number of pears, the store has sold 0.30p pears. The original number minus the number sold will equal 455.

$$p - 0.30p = 455$$

$$0.7p = 455$$

$$p = \frac{455}{0.7} = \mathbf{650\, pears}$$

23. B: Round each time to the nearest whole number and add.

$$29 + 31 + 29 + 27 + 36 = \mathbf{152}$$

24. B, D, E
   A. Corresponding angles in right triangles are not necessarily the same, so they do not have to be similar.
   B. All spheres are similar.
   C. Corresponding angles in isosceles triangles are not necessarily the same, so they do not have to be similar.
   D. Corresponding angles in a square are all the same (90°), so all squares are similar.
   E. All corresponding angles in cubes are congruent, so they are all similar.

25. E: Use the formula for percent increase.

$$\text{percent increse} = \frac{\text{amount of change}}{\text{original amount}}$$

$$= \frac{3,000}{60,000} = 0.05 = \textbf{5}\%$$

26. D: Substitute one (x, y) pair into each answer choice to find the correct equation.

27. C: Round each value and add.

$$129,113 \approx 129,000$$

$$34,602 \approx 35,000$$

$$129,000 + 35,000 = \textbf{164,000}$$

28. B: In this series, the exponents are decreasing by 1:

$$2^3, 2^2, 2^1, \underline{\quad}, 2^{-1}, 2^{-2}$$

To find the missing number, subtract 1 from the exponent.

$$2^{1-1} = 2^0 = \textbf{1}$$

29. A: p = number of pages written by Chris

$$2p = \text{number of pages written by Kim}$$

$$p + 2p = 240$$

$$p = \textbf{80}$$

30. D:

$$\{5, 11, 18, 20, 37, 37, 60, 72, 90\}$$

$$\text{median} = 37$$

$$\text{mode} = 37$$

$$\text{mean} = \frac{60 + 5 + 18 + 20 + 37 + 37 + 11 + 90 + 72}{9} = 38.89$$

The median is less than the mean.

31. B: Order the fractions by comparing the denominators.

$$\frac{1}{2} > \frac{1}{3} > \frac{1}{7} > -\frac{1}{6} > -\frac{1}{5} > -\frac{1}{4}$$

32. C: Use the equation for percentages.

$$\text{whole} = \frac{\text{part}}{\text{percentage}} = \frac{17}{0.4} = \textbf{42.5}$$

33. A: The number 3 is not irrational because it can be written as the fraction $\frac{3}{1}$

34. C: Substitute 5 for x.

$$2(5) - 5 \rightarrow 10 - 5 = \mathbf{5}$$

35. C: For the sum of two numbers to be odd, one number must be odd and the other even.

36. E: Solve using PEMDAS:

$$(32 \div 13) - (4 - 82) + 24$$
$$= (9 \div 1) - (4 - 64) + 16$$
$$= 9 - (-60) + 16 = \mathbf{85}$$

37. E: The tenths place is one place to the right of the decimal point.

38. E: Align the decimal points and add:

$$
\begin{array}{r}
14.25 \\
6.38 \\
+\,12.54 \\
\hline
\mathbf{33.17}
\end{array}
$$

39. A:

$$\frac{1}{2.5} = \frac{x}{10}$$
$$2.5x = 10$$
$$x = \mathbf{4}$$

40. E: The figure is a quadrilateral, a square, and a rectangle: it has four equal, parallel sides and four right angles.

41. A: The square root of 169 is **13**. You can check this answer by multiplying 13 by itself:

$$13 \times 13 = 169$$

42. C: Use the formula for probability.

$$\text{probability} = \frac{\text{desired outcomes}}{\text{possible outcomes}} = \frac{2\text{ cards}}{52\text{ cards}} = \frac{\mathbf{1}}{\mathbf{26}}$$

43. A: Use the order of operations:

$$(5^2 + 1)^2 + 3^3 = (25 + 1)^2 + 3^3 = (26)^2 + 3^3 = 676 + 27 = 703$$

44. A: Twenty-five students earned an F in science, and 70 students earned an A in science:

$$2(25) < 70$$

45. A: Add the number of cupcakes Michael will give to his friend and to his coworkers, and then subtract that value from 48.

# of cupcakes for his friend:

$$\frac{1}{2} \times 48 = 24$$

# of cupcakes for his coworkers:

$$\frac{1}{3} \times 48 = 16$$

$$48 - (24 + 16) = \mathbf{8}$$

46. B: Write each decimal as a fraction and compare the numerators.

47. D: Write a proportion and then solve for x.

$$\frac{40}{45} = \frac{265}{x}$$

$$40x = 11{,}925$$

$$x = 298.125 \approx \mathbf{298}$$

48. E: Assign variables and write the ratios as fractions. Then, cross multiply to solve for the number of apples and oranges sold.

$$x = \text{apples}$$

$$\frac{\text{apples}}{\text{bananas}} = \frac{3}{2} = \frac{x}{20}$$

$$60 = 2x$$

$$x = 30 \text{ apples}$$

There are 30 apples.

$$y = \text{oranges}$$

$$\frac{\text{oranges}}{\text{bananas}} = \frac{1}{2} = \frac{y}{20}$$

$$2y = 20$$

$$y = 10 \text{ oranges}$$

There are 10 oranges.

To find the total, add the number of apples, oranges, and bananas together.

$$30 + 20 + 10 = \mathbf{60} \text{ pieces of fruit}$$

49. B: Place the terms in ascending order. Because there is an even number of terms, the median will be the average of the middle two terms.

$$18, 19, 24, 27$$

$$\text{median} = \frac{19 + 24}{2} = \mathbf{21.5}$$

50. D: To find 6 less than the product of 9 and 4, set up the problem and follow PEMDAS:

$$(9 \times 4) - 6$$
$$36 - 6 = \mathbf{30}$$

Practice Test #3

To give test takers a different feel for the real exam, we have provided the second test online. Please go to the link below or scan the QR code to take practice test #3.

cirrustestprep.com/cbest-online-resources

ONLINE RESOURCES

Trivium includes online resources with the purchase of this study guide to help you fully prepare for the exam.

Flash Cards

Trivium's flash cards allow you to review important terms easily on your computer or smartphone.

Cheat Sheets

Review the core skills you need to master the exam with easy-to-read Cheat Sheets.

From Stress to Success

Watch "From Stress to Success," a brief but insightful YouTube video that offers the tips, tricks, and secrets experts use to score higher on the exam.

Feedback

Send us helpful feedback!

Access these materials at: **cirrustestprep.com/cbest-online-resources**

Dear CBEST test taker,

Great job completing this study guide. The hard work and effort you put into your test preparation will help you succeed on your upcoming CBEST exam. Thank you for letting us be a part of your education journey!

We have other study guides and products that you may find useful. Search for us on Amazon.com or let us know what you are looking for. We offer a wide variety of study guides that cover a multitude of subjects.

If you would like to share your success stories with us, or if you have a suggestion, comment, or concern, please send us an email at support@triviumtestprep.com.

Thanks again for choosing us!
Happy Testing
Cirrus Test Prep Team

Made in the USA
Las Vegas, NV
20 March 2024

87478528R00098